# FEARLESS PRESENCE

D0882145

BY ELEANOR STODDARD

**American Literary Press**
*Five Star Special Edition*
Baltimore, Maryland

# Fearless Presence

Library of Congress
Cataloging-in-Publication Data
ISBN-10: 1-56167-946-1
ISBN-13: 978-1-56167-946-1

Library of Congress Card Catalog Number:
2006909497

Design: Adele Robey, Phoenix Graphics, Inc.
Cover photo: ANC/U.S. Army
Maps: Chris Robinson

Published by

**American Literary Press**
*Five Star Special Edition*

8019 Belair Road, Suite 10
Baltimore, Maryland 21236

Manufactured in the United States of America

# CONTENTS

Foreword.................................................................v

Preface .............................................................. vii

1   Start of the Journey ................................................1

2   Overseas Duty................................................11

3   Mobilization ..............................................21

4   Trial Run...................................................33

5   Down Under .............................................43

6   Voyage to Leyte..........................................61

7   Nine Weeks in New Guinea ...................... 77

8   Full Circle....................................................93

9   Reentry....................................................115

10  Epilogue ................................................127

## MAPS

The Southwest Pacific Area ........................................48

New Guinea ..............................................................53

The Philippines...........................................................71

Leyte..........................................................................86


Source Notes  ...........................................................135

Bibliography..............................................................153

Acknowledgments ...................................................163

# FOREWORD

This book provides a splendid window into the most violent crisis of the twentieth century, World War II. More than sixty thousand American nurses served in the Army Nurse Corps during that war. Nurses worked closer to the front lines than they ever had before. Within the "chain of evacuation" established by the Army Medical Department nurses served under fire in field hospitals and evacuation hospitals, on hospital trains and hospital ships, and as flight nurses on medical transport planes. Veteran nurses, such as Nola Forrest, also served as leaders, who made the rules as they carved out the place of nurses and women in the military framework. This Army nurse's experience forced her to grow professionally and gave her the self-confidence. World War II had forever changed the face of military nursing.

The book begins with a description of Nola's upbringing and education. Her military career, with the major emphasis on her war service in the Pacific, comprises the bulk of the text. Highly relevant today, this experience of World War II has much to teach us about military preparedness and nursing organization of patient care. This work also provides an opportunity to learn about one of our chief nurse heroines, Lt. Col. Nola Forrest. Eleanor Stoddard has used primary source material and other important secondary sources to create a highly readable narrative about this wonderful Army nurse.

Constance Moore
Bethesda, Maryland
March 2005

# PREFACE

ON FEBRUARY 25, 1945, a headline in *The New York Times* proclaimed, "Heroic Nurses Get Thanks of Nation." Sixty-seven nurses who had endured almost three years of captivity after caring for the sick and wounded on Bataan and Corregidor were coming home alive. Their rescue from an internment camp in Manila was led by Lt. Col. Nola Forrest, like themselves an officer in the Army Nurse Corps. Her mission to fly her friends and colleagues to safety during an enemy attack marked the high point of her career.

The story of this wartime leader was one in a series of oral histories undertaken to capture the memories and reflections of women who were members of the U.S. armed forces in World War II. As part of this project I conducted two lengthy interviews with Nola Forrest in 1987 when she was eighty-seven years old. The tapes and transcripts of her interviews were destined for an archive along with those of thirty-seven other military women, and all of these are presently available for public reference in the California State University, Long Beach library.

My research on her career would have gone no further except that curiosity led me to look up newspaper accounts of a train wreck she encountered as well as the rescue mission in Manila. They not only verified her memories of these events but also brought such immediacy to each scene that it occurred to me other aspects of her narrative might be brought into sharper focus and form a starting point for revealing the life of an Army nurse whose contributions to Corps and country should become known.

Her account has the value of a long perspective. It encompasses a pre-World War I upbringing and education followed by seventeen years of peacetime service in the Army Nurse Corps (ANC) at home and abroad. This slow-moving and predictable existence changed abruptly with the outbreak of World War II. Nola's assignments began to move her rapidly through mobilization, nurse recruitment, military training on the home front, and duty overseas. She was promoted four times before becoming director of all the Army nurses in the Southwest Pacific Area (SWPA) just as the campaign in the Philippines was reaching a climax.

Her career paralleled the experience of other ANC leaders who found themselves acquiring administrative and public relations skills where few such skills had been required before. She undertook unprecedented tasks, notably in the Pacific war, that helped to enhance the status of Army nurses. She played her special part in this vast conflict, where events have tended to be underreported in comparison with the attention paid to the European theater by historians and other writers.

From the start of hostilities Allied policymakers gave second place priority to the requirements in the Pacific. Vast distances and impenetrable terrain made for frustrating logistical delays in the conduct of campaigns.  During land-based battles the oppressive humidity and incessant rain led to exhaustion for the troops and susceptibility to myriad tropical diseases not encountered in other theaters.

Medical staffs had to cope with the effects of unfamiliar pathogens in treating ill and severely wounded patients. Malaria exacted an unforeseen and serious toll. After doctors performed surgery or diagnosed a fever, the nurses gave follow-up care under weather conditions and equipment shortages that drained their energies.

To describe the work of these and other medical teams or place specific events in a broader context I drew on a number of secondary sources. But the overall narrative is based on a primary source: the body of Nola Forrest's spoken words. These I initially captured in two recorded oral history interviews and, as my work progressed, in twenty-five briefer, off-tape interviews to verify and amplify various statements she had made. These led her to new associations, adding information on incidents and relevant facts not mentioned earlier, enriching the full account.

Although distortions can occur in the process of recall, most of Nola's recollections seemed well fixed in her mind. Despite her age, she was able to retrieve memories from both early and more recent years. Sometimes she slipped on minor details such as the sequence of her first nursing jobs, the date of her brother's death, the number of Army nurses on duty in the fall of 1941, the length of time she spent in Australia and New Guinea, or the number of days and nights that passed during her voyage to Leyte. But the important memories of actual happenings in her life — some commonplace and some the "flash bulb" kind that are embedded during moments of strong emotion — were clearly visible to the listener as she described them. There could be no question that she was present on the scene and a participant in the action.

Even so, a detailed picture of Nola's military career would not have emerged from her interviews alone. She had saved her papers, and they were in the keeping of her nephew, Dr. Robert B. Forrest. With her permission he supplied complete copies of page after page of notices of appointment, military orders, memorandums, letters, and news clippings that provided the framework for a continuous narrative and a comparison of the testimony of her memory with documented events.

Other sources provided the background. They included a centennial history of Lake Wilson, Minnesota, the hometown of Nola's family; an official, but unpublished, history of the Desert Training Center by Sgt. Sidney L. Meller; an unpublished history of the Army Nurse Corps by Lt. Col. Pauline Maxwell; an unpublished history of nursing in the Southwest Pacific Area (SWPA) by Nola Forrest and Eileen Brady, composed at the request of the surgeon general's office in 1961; a scholarly chronology entitled *A History of the U.S. Army Nurse Corps* by Col. Mary T. Sarnecky, published in 1999; and a typewritten report to the chief of naval operations on the voyages of the USS *John Alden* by the commander of the naval armed guard aboard the ship.

To further set the scene, I consulted histories of the United States in the 1920s and 1930s and histories of American nursing; biographies of Generals George S. Patton, Jr. and Douglas MacArthur; and Gen. Dwight D. Eisenhower's *Crusade in Europe* for war mobilization. I drew on official Army, as well as popular, accounts of military campaigns in

New Guinea and the Philippines, including naval histories of the Battle of Leyte Gulf.

Two books that were invaluable in describing the role of medicine in keeping American soldiers alive and able to function were produced by historians in the U.S. Army Center of Military History. One was an official volume by Mary Ellen Condon-Rall and Albert E. Cowdrey, *Medical Service in the War Against Japan*, published in 1998, and the other a popular history, *Fighting for Life* by Albert E. Cowdrey, published in 1994. They appeared at a timely moment for explaining the chain of evacuation of battle casualties through SWPA medical checkpoints under varying combat conditions.

Three unpublished accounts of conditions in the Santo Tomas Internment Camp were consulted, two by Army nurses and one by an American Red Cross worker, all of whom lived through the ordeal. Publications included *The Santo Tomas Story* by A.V.H. Hartendorp, who wrote a secret history of the camp while incarcerated; *Santo Tomas Internment Camp* by Frederic H. Stevens, a camp leader; *We Band of Angels* by Elizabeth M. Norman; and *To the Angels* by Denny Williams, one of the nurses.

As time went on, I had access to six firsthand recollections of lower ranking Army nurses who served in New Guinea and the Philippines in different medical settings.

These women and others were subject to a medical policy in the Pacific that relegated them to rear areas as contrasted with the Mediterranean and European theaters where Army nurses worked closer to combat. In the SWPA region doctors and corpsmen worked near the scenes of fighting, sometimes under fire — in aid stations and movable hospitals — while the nurses joined them only in occupied territory. This policy was prompted by the fear of Japanese guerrilla attacks in the jungle and possible capture of the women. A change occurred, however, in October 1944 when nurses in two field hospitals received orders to serve under combat conditions during the invasion of Leyte.

Lt. Col. Nola Forrest, director of SWPA nurses, learned of this decision at the last minute. Under protest from her commanding officer, she volunteered to lead the nurses on their dangerous mission. On arrival in Leyte Gulf her group was subject to constant enemy attack from the air before they could disembark. Once on land they carried out their duties in an evacuation hospital under continuous raids, and their presence measurably improved the prospects for recovery of the patients in their care.

This marked one more step in recognition of the importance of Army nurses as part of medical teams. In 1898, during the Spanish-American War, civilian nurses were hired under contract with the Army and other organizations to tend to sick and wounded soldiers. Problems grew in administration, and Army leaders were eventually convinced of the advantage of placing nurses on a permanent staff within the Medical Department. In 1901, the Nurse Corps (female) was established by act of Congress with nurses appointed for three-year periods that could be renewed. They were the first women in modern times to serve directly on Army payrolls.

During World War I thousands of Army nurses went abroad to care for the wounded close to the scenes of battle. Their total reached 21,480 by Armistice Day, 1918. Those overseas were glamorous heroines in the eyes of the people back home, but the nurses themselves knew that they needed more official recognition. As an anomalous component of medical groups, neither officer nor enlisted, they lacked sufficient authority over the hospital corpsmen for their orders to carry weight.

After the war the Army Reorganization Act of 1920 granted nurses within the Army Nurse Corps (ANC) "relative rank" as officers from second lieutenant through captain. Nola Forrest joined the Army in 1924 with the relative rank of second lieutenant, hoping that her new employment would lead to travel.

In time she would find her career intersecting one way or another with many of the leading figures in the history of the Corps. In 1941, as the next world conflict cast its shadow over the nation, Maj. Julia Flikke, then the superintendent, brought her to Washington headquarters. As head of nursing personnel the following year Nola worked closely with the leading nurses in the office who were taking on larger duties. In July 1943, Col. Florence Blanchfield became the superintendent, and Nola Forrest, observing her skills, found her a "very diplomatic person [who] knew what she was doing ... all the avenues and all the angles. We got cooperation every place."

Under war demands even chief nurses at the hospital level were moving from concern with direct patient care to broader management issues. According to one historian, "...the chief nurse was housekeeper, mess officer and personnel officer for the nurses and responsible for orienting them to Medical Department policies and military customs and traditions."

In December 1942 new legislation authorized relative rank for Army nurses from second lieutenant to colonel and granted pay and allowances approximately equal to those of male commissioned officers. By 1944 twenty-six Army nurses had risen to the rank of lieutenant colonel.

Nola Forrest was one of these. With her adaptability she could fill the demands of more than one assignment. In 1943, as director of nurses in the Desert Training Center in California, she spent the greater part of a taxing year. Returning for the next six months to her previous post in Washington, she was soon ordered to her next assignment as director of Army nurses for the entire Southwest Pacific Area. Here she served from September 1944 to May 1945 when Army doctors sent her home with a mysterious illness incurred in the line of duty. The following year she was retired on disability.

Her life is a classic example of the power of circumstance to draw forth innate strengths and talents. Naturally at ease with people on every level, she was comfortable with herself and couldn't be bothered with hidden motives in others. She seems to have had little trouble making decisions and acting on them. Her management skills can be inferred from her record of advancement and from her calm, direct manner of describing her work.

In New Guinea, overseeing the administration of hospitals up and down the coast, she worked with chief doctors and nurses to resolve problems, preferring face-to-face meetings. She wrote, "... no quantity of written directives or exchanged correspondence was so effective as personal visits ... in learning the needs of individual hospitals."

The real proof of her leadership was her willingness to face personal danger. She participated in the nurses' field trials in the Desert Training Center, and she requested risky overseas duty at an age that almost foreclosed the possibility of such a move. A few months after her excursion to Leyte she was the logical choice to take one hundred nurses, accompanied by twenty doctors, to Manila to minister to the newly liberated captives in the Santo Tomas Internment Camp and extricate the imprisoned American nurses.

Under intense pressure to get the captive nurses to safety, she had to work with the camp bureaucracy, make quick decisions about departure, and ensure that every one of her charges was accounted for. Marie Adams, the Red Cross representative who flew out with the group, wrote to Nola, "I shall never forget your poise and your dignity and equanimity in the last tragic days at Santo Tomas nor your friendly interest in me who was not even a member of your nurse corps."

As for Nola's private life or her inmost thoughts we have little evidence. We know of her keenness for travel, her curiosity, her many friends, and her fondness for her family. We know that she was fun-loving and that she relished a social occasion. We know that she could show a highly competitive spirit at the bridge table. Those who might have shed light on her deeper side were gone from the scene by the time of my first interview.

Only after the death of his aunt on July 30, 1999 did Robert Forrest feel free to release some of her diary entries and letters. These revealed an interrupted romance with a man she had known early in her career. He reentered her life years later, and she had been on the verge of marrying him just before his mysterious death cut short their plans. When asked in an interview about a fiancé, Nola said tersely, "I don't want to talk about that."

Devoted to her friends in the Army Nurse Corps, she had known many of them in pre-war days when members served for many years as equals who shared a sense of loyalty to their calling. By law they could not be married, their numbers were small, they were moved around, and their posts frequently overlapped. Quartered together and eating together, they came to know each other well.

She was one of many leaders who helped the nurses under their direction to produce the remarkable record of military medicine in World War II. During the war medical teams saved ninety-six lives for each one hundred wounded, a ratio that could not have been achieved without dedicated nursing care. Working under demanding and perilous conditions, the Army nurses in the Pacific encountered greater challenges than those in any other theater. Not surprisingly, many were evacuated for disabilities incurred in the line of duty, Nola Forrest among them.

Nonetheless, she showed amazing endurance and, as she aged, was able to look back at a century of social change. She had survived dengue fever, a train wreck, long exposure to tuberculosis, kamikaze attacks, enemy strafing, DDT poisoning, and also cancer and fourteen broken bones. Through every trial she maintained her equanimity, and her love of adventure kept her traveling around the world into her eighties.

After a time, the events of the war receded into the distance and seemed ever more unbelievable. One day she said, "It seems like a dream. Could all that have happened? Could that have been me?"

It did and it was.

# CHAPTER 1

# START OF THE JOURNEY

Nola Forrest grew up on the prairie far from the seacoast, and she longed to explore the wider world. When she was halfway through college, she abandoned her studies and entered nurses training in the hope that a nursing career could lead to travel. Her expectations were more than fulfilled when her calling led to far-away places, breathtaking vistas, ballrooms and banquets, but she couldn't foresee the scenes of battle to which her travels would ultimately take her or the pivotal part she would play in the action.

The colonel began her story in her usual, matter-of-fact way. A small figure seated in an armchair in the sunny living room of her apartment in a military retirement home, she welcomed me graciously upon my arrival. She was wearing a long-sleeved, blue, silk dress, stockings, and pumps, in accord with the formal atmosphere of her surroundings. In answering my initial questions, she spoke in a voice with a pleasantly reassuring quality. Her manner of speech was deliberate and at the same time persuasive with a slight Midwestern inflection.

"I was born in Minnesota," she said, "and my father was editor of a newspaper and also postmaster, and my mother had been a teacher before she was married. I was the oldest of three children. I went through grade school, high school, and then I went to Macalester College in St. Paul."

More specifically, Nola Forrest was born June 19, 1900 in Lake Wilson, Murray County, in the southwestern corner of the state. Her father's family had lived in America less than twenty years when Nola arrived on the scene. In 1883 her grandfather, Dr. James Forrest, left Scotland with his oldest son, Martin, and journeyed westward across the United States to Murray County. He was drawn by land company promises of relatively cheap and fertile acreage and the chance to combine farming with his training as a physician. When he arrived, he bought a homestead plus two cows and a horse. He and Martin lived in a sod dugout several miles out of town while they built a big wooden house for the rest of the family — his wife and four children still in Scotland.

The doctor's move came at an opportune time. The Homestead Act of 1862 provided 160 acres of surveyed public land for anyone who would live on and improve the claim for five years. Some public land was also purchased by land companies, which held it on speculation. In 1879 a branch line of the Omaha Railroad was extended to Lake Wilson so that local farmers no longer had to take wheat eighty miles away to New Ulm by ox cart for grinding into flour. Neighboring markets were more accessible. Land became even more attractive, and land values rose. By this time, also, the Indians had been subdued through wars and treaties, and white settlers had a new sense of security.

Recent arrivals found themselves in a bountiful natural environment. According to a local historian, "When the first settlers came to western Murray County ... they could see before them miles and miles of endless rolling prairies The dense prairie grass was occasionally dotted by trees, scrubs and wild berry bushes, as well as a few beautiful lakes. In the spring and summer, brightly colored wild flowers broke up the monotony of the prairie landscape."

By 1883 in the midst of this primitive setting Lake Wilson was rising from the ground. Lumber and workmen poured into town for the construction of a large building containing a store on the first floor and a hotel on the second, while the third floor provided space for a school, church, and dance hall. A grain elevator was erected at the same time, and the stockmen built a stockyard next to the railroad branch line for the shipment of cattle. That year the town acquired its first post office.

The doctor finished his house, and Jane Brewster Forrest came to join her husband, bringing two younger sons, twin daughters, and a nursemaid. She settled in, and the family started farming while the doctor practiced rural medicine on the side. Every night he made each son write in a journal, which he would then read and correct.

Four years later James Forrest suddenly died from an uncertain cause, perhaps appendicitis; they never knew. A heavy snowstorm prevented medical help from reaching the farm some distance from the town. The hastily built coffin was hauled by wagon fifteen miles to the cemetery at Woodstock, and they lowered it in the snow. Family legend tells that they left the front door of the house open in their haste and kerosene froze in the lamps.

Jane Forrest decided to remain in the United States despite the urging of her relatives to return to Scotland. Within two years her older sons built a house for her in town, and she gave up the farm. Nola could remember that her grandmother was "very gentle, knew cuts of meat, and never let you know she'd had a bad day." She always wore black, and every afternoon she served tea with cookies or biscuits; her friends, knowing she was "at home," would drop in for a visit.

Her third son, Robert, grew up and married Catherine Peterson, a young woman of Danish descent. In 1900 they became the parents of Nola, then a son Robert, and thirteen years later, a daughter Marjorie.

Nola showed independence at an early age. By her account, she "took after no one." She started to read at three and "always had my nose in a book." She entered elementary school in a wooden building that housed the lower grades and later moved to a new brick school building where classes went only through the first two years of high school.

To complete the next phase of their education, Nola and some of her classmates traveled by train to Slayton, ten miles away. During her junior year she stayed from Monday through Friday with an English family whose daughter Rose was her age, returning to Lake Wilson on weekends. Her senior year she lived with a classmate in a boarding house.

In the fall of 1916, Nola Forrest and the high school valedictorian went on to Macalester College in St. Paul, a coeducational Presbyterian college founded in 1874. The president was James Wallace, a stern and impressive speaker, who conducted a mandatory course in Bible studies. His son, De Witt, who was later to found *The Reader's Digest*, had graduated and moved away by the time of Nola's enrollment.

The college eschewed fraternities and sororities but instead offered social clubs — one for men, one for women, and one for both sexes. Nola joined the mixed one. She also joined the Episcopal Church in St. Paul, which she said was almost the same as the Danish Lutheran church to which her mother belonged.

In 1917, the spring of her freshman year, the United States entered the war in Europe on the side of the Allies. As patriotic fever rose, many independent-minded American women volunteered for service overseas as ambulance drivers, relief workers, entertainers, interpreters, administrators, and, especially, nurses. The Red Cross and the Army and Navy were intensively recruiting nurses to relieve the overburdened medical staffs in the field as the sick and wounded streamed into hospitals near the lines.

One nurse who responded was Julia Stimson, who will appear later in the story. She helped to create a base hospital for the Red Cross in St. Louis, Missouri, which was to be sent overseas, and then sailed for France to staff a British hospital in Rouen. Another person who responded to the wartime pressure was Nola's high school English teacher, Suzanne Goertz, a beautiful woman who was admired by her student.

Giving up her teaching position, Miss Goertz entered the Eitel Hospital Training School for Nurses in Minneapolis. "She talked to me," Nola explained. "I had never thought of being a nurse before, but I had always wanted to travel more than anything, and I thought of nurses as having that chance. I decided to go over to Minneapolis to the Eitel school.

"My parents wanted me to finish college. My mother told me that nursing was 'hard, hard work, and you are not used to hard work.' The dean of the college even wrote a letter, asking them to get me to reconsider. But I decided I really wanted to be a nurse. I like to move around, you know."

Nola was not big and strong. She then stood a little over five feet tall and never weighed more than 115 pounds. Her blue eyes were nearsighted, and she had worn glasses since she was twelve years old. A picture shows her in profile at the time of the high school junior prom without the glasses and with her long, light hair done up in a soft bun. A few years later Nola is seen face forward in "granny" glasses, then the style, with her hair in a two side rolls.

During the war nurse recruiters sought out college women in the expectation that they could complete the training in less than the normal time. When Nola left college in 1918 to join her teacher, she had more education than the usual nursing candidate. Some nursing schools accepted trainees with only two years of high school, and even candidates for medical school were, in many cases, required to have completed only two years of college.

The school Nola entered was attached to a hospital in Minneapolis that had been established by Dr. George Eitel, a surgeon. His wife, Jeannette, ran the school in a style far more progressive than was common in many nursing schools up to that time. In earlier years nursing students were strictly disciplined and often worked 54-hour weeks. They lacked full-time teachers, walked miles each day carrying heavy trays, and moved 30-pound screens around the beds of patients. They were sometimes underfed, and their health deteriorated. In many hospitals they were treated more as servants than students mastering a discipline.

By contrast, the Eitel school treated its nurse trainees as budding professionals and almost like family members. According to Nola, they were often invited to the Eitels' lakeside summer home a few miles out of the city for good food and recreation. Here they sometimes socialized with young medical students from the hospital. Nola's class of approximately twenty-five students lived in a dormitory a few blocks from their classrooms. In wintertime they wore long, navy blue capes lined in crimson, and everyone recognized them as they walked to and from the hospital in the snow.

The hospital "... was beautifully decorated with mahogany beds for the patients and Oriental rugs on the floors. The food was served on china plates with a china teapot." But there was still plenty of hard work for the nurses with more "laying on of hands" than in today's high-tech care system. An obstetrics patient, for example, "stayed in the hospital two weeks. She was given a bath every morning and also a bedpan whenever she needed one. Before the mother nursed, her breasts were bathed in boric acid." That was several times daily. Nurses also had to bring meals three times a day to all the patients, make their beds, rub their backs, give enemas and medication, take temperatures, monitor their condition, and fill out charts. The doctors were obeyed in all respects.

In March 1921, Nola graduated from the Eitel Hospital School of Nursing with her friend Phoebe Nelson from Wood Lake, Minnesota. By this time the war had been over for almost two and one-half years. Though the trainees had somehow missed the flu epidemic that swept the country at war's end, they were prepared to handle many other kinds of cases from medical and surgical to obstetrics. That fall they were invited to stay on at the hospital as full-fledged members of the staff.

Nola was made assistant night superintendent while Phoebe had duty over the night wards. An obstetrics ward had twelve patients, and not only did a nurse have to look after the new mothers and feed them all their meals, but she also had to run back and forth to the delivery room, watching the intensity of labor pains to decide when to call the doctor. In the morning on any ward she made breakfast for everybody.

Snatching sleep in the daytime, the young nurses found one year of this regime was enough for both of them. "We decided we wanted to travel," said Nola. "Well, we had saved our money, and we started out. En route, we went to Washington State to visit an aunt of mine." This was Nola's mother's sister, pregnant at forty, and she had a goiter problem. Labor was hard, but the nurses saved the baby, and the mother survived as well.

Completing this voluntary service, the travelers embarked on their first real journey. They were escaping two unwelcome suitors, according to Nola's nephew, and they went as far as San Francisco. Here they paid a visit to "Uncle Billy" (William Forrest), a utility executive, and then found employment in a small, luxurious hospital north of the city. Nola remembered that they were two in a staff of four and they were encouraged to go to parties, enjoy themselves, and sleep late.

Just as they were becoming bored with this easygoing life, somebody told them about "a hospital in Sawtelle … looking for nurses." So they moved for the last six months of 1923 to the National Soldiers Home in Los Angeles County, marking their first experience with work in a veterans hospital.

Then "some friends of ours asked us about going into the Army. Of course, growing up in Minnesota, we didn't know anything about the Army. There happened to be an old post there, Fort Snelling, but no hospital." The fort, high on a bluff above the junction of the Mississippi and Minnesota rivers, had been established in 1819 as a protection against Indians, and Minneapolis later grew up on the site.

On January 17, 1924 the two nurses entered the Army Nurse

Corps (ANC) Reserve, "and that was the beginning of my Army career," Nola declared, even though there would be a hiatus. She and Phoebe were benefiting from a new status of "relative rank" as second lieutenants, titles that gave added authority in dealings with hospital staff.

The Army Reorganization Act of June 4, 1920 was the culmination of a campaign started three years previously by the American Nurses' Association to redefine the anomalous status of the Army nurse. Many leading women's groups, nursing leaders, and ordinary nurses joined the Association to lobby Congress for absolute rank. They were helped by the passage that same year of a Constitutional amendment giving American women the right to vote, which brought a new and significant pressure group to the attention of lawmakers. Several bills were introduced to support the nurses' initiative, and after some setbacks an act providing "relative rank" was signed into law.

Under the partial authority of relative rank Army nurses would be given the same respect as commissioned officers though receiving lower pay. They were denied the right of command and could not serve as members of a military court although they were allowed to bring charges against any member of the military. They were authorized the insignia of the grade, the privilege of the salute, and the use of the military rank title for official business — for use in documents and letters. In oral address the use of *Miss* or *Mrs.* (for widows) was indicated for first and second lieutenants. Patients could use the address *Nurse*.

The superintendent, who was promoted from captain to the relative rank of major, could sign her own official papers for the first time. Her office became the Army Nurse Corps Division, and she now reported directly to the surgeon general instead of the chief, Personnel Division, as formerly.

In 1924, Nola and Phoebe went on duty at Letterman General Hospital in San Francisco as members of the ANC reserve since no openings were available in the regular ranks. Their orders were signed by Maj. Julia Stimson, superintendent of the Army Nurse Corps. At the end of World War I she attained this position on the basis of her record as chief nurse of the American Red Cross Nursing Service and Director of Nursing for the American Expeditionary Forces in France, clarifying lines of authority between the two groups. She would head the ANC from 1919 to 1937, longer than anyone before or since.

Nola and Phoebe stayed at Letterman for a year and a half until their contract ran out, a shorter period than for appointed nurses, whose Army contracts ran for three years. At the end of their tour the two adventurers left California and returned to Washington State, but not for long. "From there," Nola recounted, "we decided we wanted to go to the East Coast. In those days there were unlimited opportunities for nurses. You could take a job; if you didn't like it, next day you could find another one."

Congress established veterans hospitals in 1919; they were very well funded, and administrators were looking for staff. Nola and Phoebe learned to call the Veterans Bureau in Washington, D.C., and inquire about openings whenever they wanted to move on. At one time they were offered work in Chicago, but turning that down, they accepted employment in another veterans hospital in Marysville, Ohio, which specialized in neuropsychiatric cases.

By 1926 the two friends were working in Castle Point, New York, in a hospital for World War I veterans afflicted with tuberculosis. Nola recalled that these were men of high caliber, mostly college graduates, and that she and Phoebe felt pain, caring for them and getting friendly, knowing they would die. The nurses stayed about a year, then served a brief stint in a private hospital where they quit in disdain because of unprofessional practices.

The young women now decided they would travel west again. "In those days trains were very comfortable with good food, porters, and maids," Nola went on. She told how she and Phoebe "would be sitting in a daytime car, and the maid would come up and say that two gentlemen had asked her to ask them if they would like to play bridge. After a bridge game, the gentlemen would treat us to dinner."

This was the golden age of American railroads. Competition was keen. In the 1920s, even though passenger traffic provided only a fraction of railroad revenue, crack passenger trains symbolized the overall capabilities of any Class I railroad. Known as Limiteds, their long trails of linked cars with company names emblazoned on the sides crossed the country in every direction.

The Pullman pool of sleeping and parlor cars could be moved rapidly from region to region to fill seasonal demands. These cars with their dark green upholstery were attended by teams of African American

8

employees, then known as colored people. More colored people worked on railroads than in any other industry, and the Pullman Company was the largest single railroad employer. The porter in the sleeping cars not only made up the berths at night, but he also carried baggage, ladders for upper berths, and extra pillows, and provided games and light refreshments during the day. He would brush suits, iron shirts, and polish shoes, if so requested.

The club car at the end of the train was spacious and furnished with swivel seats that could turn in toward the other passengers or outward toward the passing scene. One could drink sodas, write letters on railroad stationery, and use a special lounge where the ladies could escape the ubiquitous cigar smoke. In the dining car the tables were set with real linen, china, heavy silverware, and cut flowers. One could choose from an extensive menu, and a four-course steak dinner, elegantly served, cost $1.75 in 1929, a bit steep but worth the outlay.

By Nola's account she and Phoebe crossed the United States on such a train at least four times. On this last crossing, they returned to San Francisco, and the end of February 1927 saw them once again as reserve nurses on active duty at Letterman, and here they stayed. They wore white cotton uniforms and white caps, had thirty consecutive days of night duty followed by four to five months of day duty. Their work focused on ordinary medical problems — infectious diseases, chronic diseases, hernias, appendicitis, broken bones, accidental injuries, and obstetrics. In the wards everyone stood at attention when a doctor entered, even ambulatory patients. He would then say, "At ease."

At lunch one day the two friends were asked by the chief nurse, Capt. Dora Thompson, if they didn't want to join the regular Army. Miss Thompson had been superintendent of the Army Nurse Corps in World War I, was well connected, and recognized their competence. But the response she received was lukewarm. "We didn't know as we wanted to be committed that much," said Nola. "In those days we were getting seventy dollars a month in the Army, which was considerably less than other places. But we also liked the idea of travel."

Army pay scales were established by law in 1920, and the base pay of an entering ANC member of $70 per month (which could increase with time served) did not change until the Pay Readjustment Act of 1942. Civilian nurses at that time could make anywhere from $140 to $173 per month depending on the nature of their work.

"We knew that Army nurses could be sent to Panama, Puerto Pico and Hawaii and as far away as China," Nola continued, "and we had heard that people had a good time in the Philippines. So we said we would join if we could go to the Philippines. Miss Thompson had served there after the war [as assistant superintendent in the Philippine Department], and she said, 'I think I can get you to the Philippines by September.' Well then, we joined right away."

Nola's appointment as a second lieutenant in the Army Nurse Corps was dated July 18, 1927. She was by now entitled to a recently granted benefit — retirement pay based on length of service. Phoebe received a similar appointment, and both stayed on at Letterman fourteen months longer until their wish came true.

During her wandering years Nola seems to have fallen in love. The evidence is fragmentary — a notation or two in her diary and parts of eight or ten letters from a man named Mac. In July 1928 she told her diary about receiving roses from "my darling." The letters have been torn in half, as though she decided to throw them away and then changed her mind. Mac wrote of his feelings, his intense admiration, and his despair at their parting. Whatever his identity, it is clear from his words that their separation, for whatever reason, was inevitable since he declared his love forever — wherever she might be.

On September 28, 1928, Nola Forrest and Phoebe Nelson sailed for Manila on the USS *U.S. Grant* and reported for duty at Sternberg General Hospital. Nola was to enjoy "two marvelous years" in this post. She could not have imagined the chain of events that would one day bring her back to a shattered and suffering city.

# CHAPTER 2

# OVERSEAS DUTY

In 1928, America seemed to be riding the crest of a wave. For most of the decade the economy had been expanding. Despite unemployment in some sectors, the construction market was booming, new automobiles were selling rapidly, and people were speculating recklessly in financial markets. In the presidential election that November, the Republican candidate, Herbert Hoover, overwhelmingly defeated Democrat Alfred E. Smith, and prices on the New York Stock Exchange continued their climb to unprecedented heights.

And in Manila, "It was right after gold had been discovered," Nola could remember, "and everyone had a lot of money, all the civilians. We had just a wonderful time ... especially for a young person coming from the Middle West. We'd go to these seven-course dinners with a different wine for every course [no Prohibition], and we'd go to the different clubs — the Polo Club, the Manila Club, the Army and Navy Club, and the ratio of men to women was about ten or fifteen to one. So there was always something to do."

Manila was a leading commercial center in that part of the world as well as the capital of the country, the largest city and the chief port. At the time of the nurses' arrival, many representatives of U.S. firms were there to foster trade with Philippine industries. Good feeling was building with the local population under the new, more moderate administration that had recently been put in place.

The islands had been under American rule since the Spanish American War of 1898, and the United States had maintained a continuous military presence there. Trade grew with the islands, and free trade was established in 1909, making the Philippines almost entirely dependent on the American market. But the question of independence for the Philippines remained a burning issue in both U.S. and local politics.

At home the Democrats came to power in 1912, and steps were taken to prepare the Philippines for self-rule. Congress passed the Jones Act, which provided for a popularly elected upper house with power to approve all the appointments of the governor general. The measure gave the islands a definite pledge of independence, although the starting date was left indefinite.

In 1921, when a Republican administration regained control, Gen. Leonard Wood was appointed governor general. He had formerly commanded U.S. military forces in the islands, and he instituted semimilitary rule, reversing the policy of bringing Filipinos into the government to prepare them for the future. His reforms antagonized influential legislators, whom he overrode by abolishing the cabinet. Unrest was widespread in the Philippines until Wood's death in 1927.

That year President Calvin Coolidge appointed Henry L. Stimson (first cousin of Julia Stimson) as Wood's successor. The new administrator softened many formerly harsh policies and aimed to reestablish the governing of the Philippines as a cooperative enterprise. He worked tactfully to modernize laws affecting corporations, banks, and landholders in order to attract American capital and stimulate the economy.

During his term in office he became fast friends with Gen. Douglas MacArthur, the newly appointed commander of the Philippine Department of the U.S. Army. The general made another close friend in Manuel Quezon, leader of the local Nationalista party, who was a frequent guest in his home. The friendships of these three men would carry over into a time of war when their altered roles might bring them, if possible, even closer.

In those days Manila residents lived a slow-paced and pleasurable life. The narrow coastal plain of Luzon, lying against a backdrop of volcanic mountains and dense forests, offered a hot, humid, and enervating climate with frequent tropical rainstorms. Within this setting the city was alive with many contrasts. Modern areas contained hospitals, universities, office buildings, movie theaters, night clubs, and parks while nearby stood centuries-old churches, monasteries, slums, and nipa huts. Street cars, buses, automobiles, and pony carts ran endlessly between myriad points of business and diversion.

The old portion of Manila was named the Intramuros, or Walled City, a relic of Spanish rule. It was located on the south bank of the Pasig River. The Malacanan, the palatial residence of the governor general, with its lush gardens, also faced the river on that side. On the north bank of the river, the newer parts of the city included the commercial district, a host of clubs, and such social centers as the Manila Hotel, with its big outdoor patio for evening parties.

Aside from dining and dancing in the various ballrooms, military officers could bowl, swim, and play tennis. Golf was a major attraction, available on the course at Fort McKinley a few miles outside of town. The status of relative rank for Army nurses included among their privileges full access to officers' clubs and sports facilities. As single women they could be much in demand for social events, but if one of them married, she would have to resign from the service.

At Sternberg General Hospital the routine allowed ample time for outside activities. Nola had 12-hour night duty or 6-hour day duty, which ran either from six to noon or twelve to six. Along with the other nurses she wore a white uniform and cap although there was no requirement for uniforms off duty. She wrote home that "the work was much the same as the States with the addition of tropical diseases." Local citizens received treatment along with the military. In the course of her work Nola became acquainted with two people who would enter her life again — a nurse named Martha Jane Clement and a young Army surgeon named Norman T. Kirk.

The nurses' dormitory was right across from the hospital. "We are situated in a very nice part of the city," Nola told her family, "and have lovely quarters although they look very strange to us. Everything is so bare — no rugs on the floor, no windows, no shades — to obtain maximum coolness ... Our rooms are built on little patios, all opening to the porch ... We have bars on the bottoms and tops of the beds and have to sleep under mosquito nets to prevent the dengue mosquito from biting [and] we have to keep carbon lights burning in our closets to keep our clothes from getting moldy."

In the kitchen a Chinese cook made superb meals and would pre-pare a special order for breakfast on mornings when a nurse slept late. A houseboy answered the phone downstairs and admitted callers. When one of Nola's escorts arrived in the dayroom, the houseboy would come to her door and say, "Someone is calling you down."

The manners of that "someone" were likely to be courteous and a bit protective. The men who sought the nurses' company were gentle-manly and solicitous. If a group was seated around a table in a restau-rant, one of the men would always ask, "Who has duty at six?" To who-ever raised her hand, he would say, "No drinks for you tonight."

In this idyllic setting was a marriage proposal likely? Of course. The representative of the New York Life Insurance Company, a man named Johnson, wanted Nola to marry him. She was tempted, and she thought about it. But she decided that living in Manila permanently with a month to travel home by ship and a month to wait for mail from home detracted from the prospect. She declined and may thereby have avoided becoming a prisoner of war in December 1941 when the Japanese occupied the city.

During her tour Nola was able to see more of the world, but her friend Phoebe was not so lucky. She had been in Manila little more than half a year when she was diagnosed with tuberculosis, contracted in a veterans hospital, and was shipped back to the States for treatment. Meanwhile Nola saved her leave to take a long vacation. Army nurses were entitled to a paid leave of absence at the rate of thirty days for each calendar year of service, and could accumulate these for as much as 120 days.

From May 11 to June 24, 1929, Nola joined three other nurses on a voyage to Japan and China. Landing in Yokohama, they moved on to the Imperial Hotel in Tokyo where, Nola wrote, they "were impressed by the rose taffeta bedspreads and drapes and the beautiful green sunken bathtub." They went on to see Mt. Fuji and then to visit Nikko where they spent the night in a native Japanese inn, tied in kimonos and sleeping on mats.

Nola wrote that Japan was "a beautiful, lovable little country and even if the Japs are willing to knife us in the back (as I guess they are) nevertheless their politeness is extremely gratifying." Her use of the terms *Japs* reflected even then an underlying racial distain for these people on the part of Americans. This feeling would be later intensified by wartime propaganda depicting them as hateful savages, and "buck-toothed, bespectacled lunatics," subhuman in nature, reciprocated by equally disparaging images of Americans on the part of the Japanese.

Nola's party sailed across the Yellow and Inland Seas and up the China Coast to Tientsin and Peking. Boarding a homeward boat at Taku, they went as far as Darien in Manchuria where they were driven around in 4-wheeled droshkies. The next stop was Shanghai for shopping, then on to Hong Kong with its spectacular harbor and back to Manila.

Upon her return Nola was stricken with dengue fever, a common affliction in the tropics. Transmitted by the bite of a small mosquito, it was known as "break bone" fever, producing a very high temperature, agonizing aches in head and joints, a state of prostration and a miserable rash. Within a fortnight she shook it off.

A few months later she set out on another voyage, this time for ten days of detached duty in the Southern Islands, a not unpleasant assignment. Embarking on a small tropical boat with an upper deck veranda, she and another nurse were the only women among a group of American businessmen who were stopping off at various ports to close commercial deals.

Their craft called at a number of Philippine islands, including Samar, Cebu, Iloilo, Zamboanga, and Dumaguete. Social life was lively; Nola remembered a Chinese feast served one morning at 2:00 a.m., and a visit to the Sultan of Sulu in the Sulu Archipelago at the southwestern tip of the island group. The ruler entertained his guests in a moth-eaten palace where they were treated to canned fruit served right out of the can.

Back in the United States the economic climate was darkening. In October 1929 the long bull market ended with a crash. A recession that had begun in construction and automobile output a few months earlier continued to deepen and spread to other industries. The next year the government took the first census of unemployment and found five million out of work.

Yet the national crisis had little effect on the enclosed world of the Army Nurse Corps. The nurses remained in their jobs, although the appointment of every member was renewed periodically. In February 1930, Nola requested "continuation of service," as was the rule, through channels that went up to the surgeon general's office. Soon Major Stimson's signature appeared on a memo approving her continuation in the Corps for another three years.

In military circles these were quiet times. During the previous decade pacifist sentiment swept the nation and its allies. In 1922 the Washington Conference resulted in several treaties that set different ratios of capital ships between Great Britain, the United States, Japan, France, and Italy, and outlawed the use of poison gas. In 1928 the Kellogg-Briand Pact bound fifteen nations to "renounce war for the solution of international controversies." In 1930 the London Naval Conference produced another set of ratios between the United States, Great Britain, and Japan in small cruisers and destroyers and parity in submarines.

As the recession intensified, public thinking focused on the economy and domestic issues. In September 1930, General MacArthur returned to the States to assume new duties as chief of the general staff of the U.S. Army, and for the next five years he would find the military had little influence on foreign policy. He had to battle with Congress to win support for the one hundred and thirty thousand enlisted men and twelve thousand officers under his authority.

Isolationist feeling brought passage of the first Neutrality Law in 1935, followed by a second one in 1936 and still another in 1937. Even as waves of aggression swept Europe and Asia, these measures taken together prohibited American vessels from carrying arms to or for belligerents in any foreign war, forbade the granting of loans to belligerents, and even empowered the U.S. president to apply these terms to foreign civil wars.

Nola's career was entering a quiet phase that reflected the general slowdown. In October 1930 she made a change of station with orders "to proceed, via Government transportation through the Panama Canal to New York City." Overseas duty for Army nurses lasted only two years as compared with domestic duty, which could be extended for any length of time. Nola had three months' leave of absence and visited her parents before reporting to Walter Reed General Hospital in Washington, D.C., in January 1931.

After the leisurely routine in Manila, this new assignment was a backbreaker. "I had to take the place of three head floor nurses who went on vacation three months in a row," said Nola. She decided to ask Capt. Julia Flikke, assistant superintendent of the Army Nurse Corps, for a transfer to Fitzsimons General Hospital in Denver, Colorado. This hospital cared for all the Army patients with tuberculosis, and here her friend Phoebe Nelson was undergoing treatment.

In mid-April, Nola Forrest made her move to Fitzsimons. She stayed there for five years, working directly with patient care, conducting pneumothorax procedures for the collapse of lungs and carrying out ward duties, administering narcotics, maintaining charts, and directing the corpsmen. She had tea one day in Denver with Major Stimson, who was visiting on one of her inspection trips. The ANC superintendent asked her why she wasn't a chief nurse. Nola explained that she preferred to be a head nurse over the wards, maintaining her contact with the patients.

As the months and years went by, she watched Phoebe slowly regain her strength. Before the discovery of antibiotics the only treatment for TB was enforced inactivity, good food, fresh air, and hope. Even in the coldest weather the patients were bundled up and put on outdoor verandahs for much of the day.

When she was finally able to leave the hospital, Phoebe succumbed to the entreaties of a suitor named Karolchnik whom she had known in Manila. Nola remembered how he met them when they first arrived in the city. He laid claim to Phoebe and got a friend of his to take both of the women up in an airplane over the harbor. Nola wryly remarked that this was the only time in her life she was ever really frightened.

Phoebe married Karolchnik, unaware that he had given a ring to a nurse in Manila. Having distrusted him from the start, Nola could muster no enthusiasm for her friend's decision. Phoebe moved with her husband to Baguio in the mountainous region of northern Luzon and there gave birth to a daughter. She soon found, however, that her husband was spending most of his time in Manila, 160 miles away, while he pursued his liaison with the nurse. She sent for her mother and sister to keep her company.

After a while Phoebe, having saved some of the pay accumulated during her illness, plotted with her family to escape. She hired a taxi to take them to Manila where they boarded a ship bound for Portland,

Oregon, without her husband's knowledge. There Phoebe became a real estate agent and was able to divorce her husband. He never provided support for his daughter, but one day without warning he sent her a grand piano.

Meanwhile Robert Forrest, Nola's brother, had purchased a newspaper, the *Pocahontas Democrat*, and moved to Iowa. He had gained publishing experience working with his father on the *Lake Wilson Pilot* in his hometown. Getting his paper reestablished, he overworked a heart already damaged by rheumatic fever, and in April 1935 he was stricken with a heart attack.

To reach him Nola flew on her first commercial plane ride from Denver to Des Moines, where she was met by her parents. They drove to Pocahontas, but by the time they joined his family, her brother had died. As the funeral procession drove to the cemetery, she remembered the people of the town lining both sides of the street to show their respect.

This marked a sad end to Nola's tour of duty at Fitzsimons, which came a few months later. She was fortunate not to have contracted TB, although she claimed she had scars on her lungs. During her five years at this hospital her vacations were limited in scope. She purchased a Ford and drove to points of interest in Colorado, New Mexico, and other parts of the West, but there were no ocean voyages. On many posts Army nurses had access to sports, horseback riding, dancing, bridge games, and movies, but Nola remembered Fitzsimons more for work than play.

In the period from the mid-1920s to the late 1930s the number of Army nurses hovered between 675 and 825 on active duty. Small numbers and long retention promoted the growth of lasting friendships. As the economy weakened, the Nursing Division received many applications from unemployed civilian nurses, who would at this time receive less pay than those in the Army. Their chances of acceptance were slim since Reserve nurses had first call and the waiting list was long.

Most nurses remained in the Corps because they would not be able to find jobs outside, or the security. The opportunity also existed for transfer to a better station, perhaps to a foreign post, and this is what happened to Nola Forrest. In February 1936 she was ordered to Hawaii. She sailed from San Francisco for Honolulu, taking her car with her.

After a 6-day voyage on an Army transport, she reported on the 11th of March at Schofield Barracks on the island of Oahu.

This was the largest Army post in Hawaii and, indeed, the Army's largest base worldwide. During the Spanish American War, the commanding general of the Army was John M. Schofield, who pushed for annexation of Hawaii in 1898 and thereafter for placing a military reservation on a portion of the Leilehua Plain in central Oahu. From such a base, he argued, the Army could move with speed to protect Pearl Harbor and the rest of the Oahu shoreline.

In 1909 facilities were constructed on fifteen thousand acres for men and equipment, and the base was named for the general. At the time of Nola's arrival, Schofield Barracks had grown into "a small city with its own streets, parks, shopping center, cemetery, bank, post office, theater, sports arena, school and churches," according to an article in *Honolulu* magazine. It was considered the most beautiful base in the U.S. Army with its mountainous backdrop, green vegetation, and blue-rimmed shoreline.

Here Nola's duties resembled those in Sternberg General Hospital except that shifts were different — three hours in the morning with some time off, then another three hours in the afternoon. Along with the work, the station provided many benefits. The nurses lived in their own quarters with servants to take care of the housekeeping. They had a Japanese cook, who prepared excellent food and did wonders with coconut. Upon reflection Nola suspected he might have been a spy.

With her love of a good time she spent many of her leisure hours outside her quarters. She had an active social life as the only nurse in a social group of fourteen people — six male engineers and their wives plus a bachelor doctor and herself. The doctor was "just a friend," and that was fine with her, as later events could explain. She remembered frequent parties and bridge games and swimming in clear water in beautiful weather.

During her tour she and another nurse forsook their assigned quarters and rented a cottage at the beach. They would rise at 5:00 a.m., drive up to the hospital, put in their hours, and be back at the cottage by late afternoon for a swim. They entertained on numerous occasions, enjoying a pleasantly balanced life.

By this time Army nurses were no longer required to renew their contracts. Now a permanent member of the Corps, Nola served, as always, at the discretion of the Medical Department. On March 16, 1938, just two years from the date of her arrival at Schofield Barracks, she was reassigned to the station hospital at Fort Lewis, Washington.

She had two months' leave of absence before her change of station, a baffling period which began with joy and ended in sorrow. Somehow during the intervening years Mac had reentered her life, and Nola was planning to marry him. After a rousing send-off from her friends — one said "Never saw so many leis" — Nola sailed for the States to meet her fiance. No record exists of the courtship or its abrupt finale, but nine letters of condolence, most dated April 1938, were saved, and they reveal the heartbreaking fact of Mac's unexpected death.

One letter from Ann in Beverly Hills, "I have thought of you no end of times since I saw you last, so radiant and happy. Only experiences like your own can show ... how strangely and swiftly our lives can be stripped to grief."

Three notes from Schofield Barracks are typical but give few hints of the details — Gus: "It is so tragic, and just when you were planning to be so happy. He was so young and promising to go so soon"; Lucile: "I've wanted happiness for you and I was sure when you got to the Mainland that everything would be all right. You will always have the memory of seeing him, even for a short time ..." ; LaDonna: "I still cannot believe it ...I had no idea where to cable you as you mailed the letter in El Paso ... There's one thing, you were with him, and that must have meant a lot to you both ... [here] ... the usual parties, the same people, same partners, same dresses, same food, same cocktails and same, same, but that's army."

No account remains of how or where Mac died — or even a reference to his last name. Nola refused to speak about him when asked in an interview if she had been engaged, but she kept the letters of sympathy from her friends. Her living relatives, a nephew and two nieces, can add nothing to the perplexing words in the letters.

During the rest of her leave, mostly spent with her family, she mustered the strength to put this dream and this memory behind her, although she did not quite erase the paper trail. Had she married, her career with the Corps would have been finished. Since it was far from finished, her story can move on.

# CHAPTER 3

# MOBILIZATION

N ola Forrest arrived at Fort Lewis, Washington, in May 1938 before most Americans understood that the spread of Naziism abroad could seriously affect their lives. They knew that Adolph Hitler was building a war machine, and in the newsreels they had recently seen German troops march in and occupy neighboring Austria. Yet in September of that same year Great Britain and France signed the Munich Pact ceding the Sudetenland on the western border of Czechoslovakia to Germany as a measure that promised to guarantee peace.

Against this background Fort Lewis reflected a slowly awakening response to events across the seas. This was the largest Army center in the northwest, located halfway between Tacoma and Seattle on Puget Sound. In 1937 a month of maneuvers by troops from several western states, who made up the 3d Infantry Division, had ended here in a massed review. The review was commanded by Brig. Gen. George C. Marshall, then in charge of the division's 5th Brigade at Vancouver Barracks in Washington.

A detachment of the division at Fort Lewis consisted of only two thousand men, but their ranks were destined to grow. In March 1938 eighteen hundred men of the 15th Infantry Regiment were added to the garrison forces when the regiment returned from a 25-year tour of duty in Tientsin, China. Nola remembered the atmosphere as fairly quiet when she came, even though troop strength was growing and several hundred new structures were springing up around the grounds.

Determined not to brood, she found outside activities. She had brought her car with her from Hawaii, and she took weekend excursions around the state and up into British Columbia where she spent a festive Christmas holiday at the Empress Hotel in Victoria.

She soon saved enough time to take a lengthy annual leave. In the fall of 1939 a 36-day vacation found her traveling south with her friend Lucile, who had come from Oahu for the trip. First they visited the Golden Gate International Exposition in San Francisco, followed by visits to Los Angeles and San Diego, and over the border to Tijuana in Mexico.

Since an extended itinerary was typical of Nola's zest for adventure, the two tourists continued on, crossing the country by train to New Orleans, dropping in on friends. They next turned north and, as the culmination of their vacation, visited the New York World's Fair. They spent their nights in the city at the Barbizon Plaza Hotel, which catered exclusively to women, and each morning boarded a chartered bus for the fairgrounds at Flushing Meadows on Long Island.

The exposition was aptly named the World of Tomorrow. Sixty nations displayed their specialized products and indigenous talents in colorful exhibits. In the center of the grounds the 610-foot Trylon and the huge Perisphere globe dominated the landscape. The travelers, after strolling past the Lagoon of Nations, might glide on an elevated conveyor belt through the General Motors Futurama with its miniature superhighways carrying a steady stream of model cars from coast to coast; or see themselves on the first TV screens; or make a free long-distance phone call while everybody listened; or see fluorescent lighting and fax machines; or have their pictures taken in Technicolor. In the midst of such marvels of technology they joined crowds that were in a buoyant and hopeful mood.

On the other side of the Atlantic Ocean war had broken out, and some countries hastily closed down their exhibits. In the spring, Hitler had seized control of the whole of Czechoslovakia, and late in August he concluded a 10-year nonaggression pact with the Soviet Union, allaying a threat from the east. At dawn on September 1st he invaded Poland, and two days later Great Britain and France jointly declared war on Germany.

Watching from a distance, Americans for the most part were determined to stay out of the hostilities even though Congress passed a law repealing the arms embargo in favor of a "cash and carry" system that helped the Allied powers. But contrary to prevailing opinion, some military officers could read the signs that a global conflict was in the offing. "I was certain that the United States would be drawn into the whirlpool of the war," Gen. Dwight D. Eisenhower stated in his book *Crusade in Europe.*

He was stationed during the late 1930s in Manila as chief of staff for Gen. Douglas MacArthur, who headed a military mission to build a defense force for the Philippine government in anticipation of independence. As soon as the European war erupted, Eisenhower requested permission to leave the islands.

In early 1940 he was placed on detached service in California to assemble the far-flung troops of the IX Corps area. In the entire nation five hundred and four thousand men were on active duty or in the trained reserves. The Army was eighteenth in size worldwide. Eisenhower described the mass of U.S. Army officers and men at that time as "[lacking] any sense of urgency. Athletics, recreation, and entertainment took precedence in most units over serious training."

Training was limited to the unit level; field exercises were not undertaken. Infantrymen, few in number, lacked weapons and equipment, and many carried ineffective wooden models of mortars and machine guns. Even their Springfield rifles were obsolete. Eisenhower was soon assigned to Camp Ord on the Monterey Peninsula where he helped to lead the 15th Infantry Regiment in the practice of so-called "war games."

Medical teams from Fort Lewis and other Army posts went there to expand the capacity of the station hospital at the Monterey Presidio, and Nola Forrest came with her group. She remembered the way the head doctor welcomed the nurses, who he thought could help with hysterectomies for Army wives. His focus shifted when the troops on maneuvers were stricken throughout the ranks with poison ivy.

"The nurses' quarters were right next to the administration building," Nola recalled, "and we could raise our shades at night and see the chief officers, like Eisenhower and General Marshall [recently appointed Army chief of staff], conferring into the night and pointing with their wands at big charts on the wall." In May 1940 she returned to Fort Lewis.

During that spring the countries of western Europe were falling swiftly under Nazi domination. In April, German armies, after thrusting into Norway and Denmark, launched a shattering offensive against Belgium and Flanders and pushed on into northern France. Late in May the British had to evacuate three hundred and thirty-eight thousand Allied soldiers trapped at the French port of Dunkirk to England in small ships under heavy fire.

As France weakened against the enemy, Italy declared war on France and Great Britain. On June 21st, France was forced to surrender to Germany, and the country was divided into two zones — one occupied and one unoccupied. With the news of these events the attitudes of opinion leaders in the United States started to shift. Some authorities who had opposed the country's entrance into the conflict began to think that economic aid alone would not save Great Britain from defeat. These fears were heightened when Hitler launched an all-out air attack on southeast England as a preliminary to invasion.

Listening on thirty million radios to war bulletins from London and Berlin, Americans felt the danger and uncertainty with an immediacy not conveyed by press accounts. In mid-1940 a Roper poll revealed that more than one-half of the public expected an Axis victory yet an even larger share favored a reimposition of the draft.

In August a congressional resolution authorized the President to call up the National Guard along with the organized reserves, and the Guard soon appeared on the scene at Fort Lewis. The new troops were part of the famed Rainbow Division, which had arrived first in France in World War I and fought with distinction under General MacArthur.

Public opinion enabled President Franklin D. Roosevelt to help England in September with fifty outmoded U.S. destroyers in exchange for the lease of nine Western Hemisphere bases. That same month Congress passed the Selective Service and Training Act of 1940. Signed into law, it obligated draftees between the ages of twenty-one and thirty-five for an induction period of one year for service only in the Western Hemisphere. In November Roosevelt was reelected for a third term in the wake of growing war anxieties.

Fort Lewis began absorbing a stream of troop arrivals, as many as twenty-six thousand by Christmas. In the fall the 41st Infantry Division had arrived in the area with twelve thousand officers and men, who were housed in "winterized" tents with wooden floors and plank side walls. Every day new installations appeared on the landscape.

In the nation public thinking remained ambivalent. As the year began, most Americans favored rearmament but were inclined to feel that a real engagement abroad or the threat of an enemy attack could be dismissed as unlikely. The holiday season found many civilians in an upbeat frame of mind. The Depression was easing, partly from increased military spending, and people were finding jobs, buying new clothes and extravagant gifts, and seeking entertainment.

Nola remembered that "Temporary barracks were mushrooming all over the place, and I helped to open a new station hospital to take care of the 41st Division." As chief nurse she was promoted to first lieutenant in February. She could remember Mamie Eisenhower and son John coming into the dispensary. Colonel Eisenhower had returned to his regular assignment at the Fort, where he had access to training funds that enabled his 15th Infantry Regiment and the National Guard to go on extended field maneuvers. He soon became chief of staff of the IX Corps, reassigned to Fort Lewis.

"During the spring of 1941," he wrote, "every post and camp was astir with the business of building the Army of the United States. The entire West Coast area was in a state of almost endless movement—men arriving in groups ... cadres of men being withdrawn to form new organizations ... cities of tents and barracks with all the multiple utilities of modern living—hospitals, water systems, light and power plants—springing up overnight where before there had been open fields."

In March the President signed the controversial Lend Lease Act, which enabled him to transfer munitions and supplies to Great Britain and other Allies on the understanding that the loan of such material would be repaid in kind at war's end. Then, as the outlook abroad grew more menacing, the President proclaimed an unlimited national emergency. He argued that the nation was clearly threatened and the best way for America to avoid entering the conflict was to become "the arsenal of democracy."

That July, Nola was transferred to Walter Reed Army General Hospital in Washington, D.C., where she stayed just two months before Maj. Julia Flikke, by now superintendent of the Army Nurse Corps, moved her to the Nursing Division within the surgeon general's office. There she worked on personnel with three fellow officers and a clerical staff of twenty. Nurses over forty years of age were likely to be sought for administrative duties. Nola was forty-one years old, and she would never again be assigned to a hospital.

A number of private and government nursing groups had been working on plans for the recruitment of Army nurses. The Red Cross Nursing Service regularly maintained a first reserve register of nurses willing to serve in the military in an emergency. The first woman from this list to go on active duty was sworn in on October 8, 1940, and by the end of the year the Army Nurse Corps had 1,371 members.

But even though age and physical requirements were eased and the Army began accepting nurses without Red Cross affiliation, inductions were falling short of established goals. By June 30, 1941, a total of 5,433 Army nurses were on duty, but many more were needed. Thousands more were enrolled in the Red Cross first reserve, but were slow to volunteer their services.

During the fall the work in the office was very light, as Nola remembered, a period of deceptive calm. Washington was built on a swamp, and the atmosphere tended to be sticky and hot except in winter. "All you had were probably a retirement or a discharge or maybe a transfer, but there was very little to do. But then December 7th came along, and [everything] changed just dramatically."

That Sunday, Nola Forrest was enjoying her weekly bridge game, which happened to be at the French Embassy where one of the players was on the staff. When the news of the Japanese attack on Pearl Harbor streamed over the radio, the four women abandoned their game and hurried home. Nola's boss, a colonel, called her and told her the extent of the disaster. A few minutes later he called back and, concerned about security, said, "Forget everything I told you."

The next day Japanese planes attacked the Philippines where the U.S. Army Forces in the Far East (USAFFE), a new command, had been established under MacArthur earlier that year. American air and naval bases were smashed, including the entire bomber command deployed on the ground at Clark Field north of Manila. Casualties flooded the hospitals in Luzon.

That same day Congress declared war on Japan and quickly

Nola Gladys Forrest, age 3
(family photo)

Nola, age 14 (family photo)

Nola on graduation from the
Eitel Hospital Training
School for Nurses, 1921
(family photo)

Nola at Castle Point, NY, 1927
(Nola Forrest papers)

Julia Stimson awarded the Distinguished Service Medal by Gen. John. J. Pershing, Tours, France, June 5, 1919 (National Archives)

Nola's letter of assignment to the Army Nurse Corps, January 17, 1924 (Nola Forrest papers)

Nola Forrest and Phoebe Nelson, 1928 (Nola Forrest papers)

Capt. Dora Thompson, assistant superintendent, Army Nurse Corps, 1920-1932 (ANC/U.S. Army)

Manila street, early 1930s
(LTC Shawn Welch)

Nurses relaxing in quarters, Manila,
1928 (ANC/U.S. Army)

Nursing staff, Sternberg General Hospital, Manila, 1929 (Nola second
from right, second row) (Nola Forrest papers)

Nursing Staff, Ft. Lewis Hospital #3, 1941 (Nola standing extreme right) (Nola Forrest papers)

Col. Julia O. Flikke, superintendent Army Nurse Corps, 1937-1943 (ANC/U.S. Army)

Col. Florence A. Blanchfield, superintendent, later chief, Army Nurse Corps, 1943-1947 (ANC/U.S. Army)

extended the term of service for military personnel to the duration and six months. Army strength then stood at one and one-half million men, including a Medical Department of over one hundred and thirty thousand members, of whom some seven thousand were nurses.

Nurses had been in demand throughout the previous year to staff Army general hospitals that were expanding as well as to meet the needs of hospitals in the training camps springing up all over the country. As nurses were moved from ward to ward to make up for staff shortages, doctors complained about the poor quality of care. In the first six months of 1942, even though almost six thousand more nurses were appointed to the Corps, this number did not make up for the drain on available staff.

Domestic requirements yielded to those of foreign theaters that had priority on staff and equipment. The government could call up civilian reserve hospitals, known as affiliates, which were established in World War I. Almost eighty of these base hospitals had been organized by collaboration between the Army Medical Department and the American Red Cross. Destined for overseas duty, they drew on personnel of large university hospitals across the country because, as an historian explained, "[t]heir inherent sense of staff cohesion combined with their advanced state of professional training would enable quicker mobilization and more efficient medical service."

"We had many reserve hospitals," said Nola, "like those at Yale, Harvard, Johns Hopkins and Mayo's. They would become part of the Army [when] they were called. A general reserve hospital had to have a hundred nurses, twenty doctors, and then so many corpsmen. The hospitals had their names, like 'the 16th General.' Some of them had [been given] their names as reserve hospitals in World War I, and they were proud of them."

As American troops began shipping out to fight a two-ocean war, reserve hospitals might be called up without a full complement of personnel. "Maybe they didn't have enough nurses to make their quota," Nola explained, "and so the Army could supply the rest of them, you see. With our small group of Army nurses, a lot of them would have had to be assigned as chief nurses to [these] units because they were the only ones that knew about the Army. And they didn't know much because we hadn't had too much training. We had very little training in administration."

By the autumn of 1942 more than eighty affiliated units had been activated, and those that were not overseas were either in training in the United States or waiting to be alerted for a move to a training camp. They received nurses from a reserve pool, and they were supplied with enlisted corpsmen from Army training units. In some cases whole training units were sent overseas in hospitals hastily brought to authorized strength with personnel from elsewhere. Such groups might meet each other for the first time as they were shipping out.

On April 1, 1942, Nola became a captain, and then assistant superintendent and head of personnel. "They started promoting," she said. "They promoted the chief [Julia Flikke] ... still relative rank, but she was promoted to colonel [in March 1942]." In three years "I was first lieutenant, captain, major, and lieutenant colonel ... real fast! Well, they just had to have you and your position called for that rank."

The Army Nurse Corps headquarters in Washington, D.C., was uprooted for the second time in just over a year to accommodate added staff and filing cabinets. "We moved, the surgeon general's office did," Nola remembered, "to 1818 H Street, took over that building across from the Roger Smith Hotel. It was a big building, and we moved in the middle of the night. Maj. [Florence] Blanchfield [deputy to Flikke] stayed behind in the old office, and I received the files in the new office. That was before we'd got very many more people into the office, and it was really a nightmare. As soon as we could, we got more help. We had to get so many secretaries and stenographers to do all this paperwork. I had one assistant who did nothing but answer inquiries from Congress."

An incessant struggle went on to keep track of assignments, shipping orders, and clothing issues. "You had to know which port to get [them] out of," Nola went on, "and that wasn't all. You see, we had to buy uniforms and decide colors, shapes, sizes, and so forth, and shoes. [The standard uniform at the start of the war was white for ward duty, regulation blue for outdoors, and blue seersucker for the tropics.] We went through several phases before we finally got what we wanted.

"One person who helped us a lot was Dorothy Shaver, who was president of Lord & Taylor. She showed us uniforms she had designed for people in the tropics, a brown and white seersucker that tied, and then pants and tops for the airevac nurses and the nurses on hospital trains."

Colonel Flikke decided to send Nola and one assistant on the

Army War Show to display the new uniforms and drum up nurse recruitment. The show was organized by Army public relations to tour the country and keep the public engaged. The tour had already started when the nurses came aboard in the summer of 1942. The itinerary was set for Pittsburgh, Akron, Detroit, Milwaukie, and Omaha, holding 4- to 10-day stands. The show comprised two thousand men from every branch of the service and two women: Capt. Nola Forrest and 1st Lt. Edna Traeger.

"By that time," Nola could state, "we already had quite a few uniforms. We had the parkas and everything for Alaska, and we had most of the uniforms they would wear here on duty, and then some of the tropical ones. And we started to recruit — that was part of it, to get plenty of nurses in. We started out in Pittsburgh, and then we went to a number of cities and on to Chicago and were ten nights at Soldier Field and filled it every night, 100,000 people, and they all paid over a dollar apiece. It was a wonderful show, just wonderful!"

A Detroit newspaper reporter wrote that the show was as good as a circus and better managed:

> There were cavalry with and without horses, airplanes, dispatch riders, riflemen, ordnance division personnel, artillery, a hospital corps, Army cooks and cookery, barbers, tanks, ambulances, religious displays, German and Japanese planes, field telephones, M.P.s, trucks, sappers, engineers, and a fellow who plays a mouth organ ... The encampment is as neat as Aunt Miranda's sewing basket. The tents run in long rows, every cot is aligned, every blanket folded, every rifle clean, every pair of shoes shined, every private shaved, every officer as calm as a bowl of porridge.

As for the nurses, "We had nothing to do with the show," said Nola, "except at night they had the biggest spotlight over the reviewing stand, and we were brought up, and we had to sit in a command car in our uniforms. But we also had to be in the back when they had the battle." A mock battle between the Japanese and the Americans, replete with fireworks and the Army band, was a major feature.

Entertainment was also offered by civilian celebrities, including such talent as Leon Leonides, manager of the Radio City Music Hall Rockettes, and Blevins Davis, the radio scriptwriter. A military celebrity was Bert Parks, by then a sergeant with Army Radio.

An article about the nurses appeared in the October 1942 issue of *R-N.* The reporter, who interviewed them in their tent at Soldier Field, called the show the "biggest publicity stunt of all times" and said that here was "a chance to tell large slices of the public that the Army nurse is very much a part of the Army."

She described Nola as "small, fair-haired, fortyish and merry" and declared that the nurses, attired in smartly tailored summer beige were "obviously enjoying their assignment." They answered innumerable questions from the crowds that rolled in, while fending off people who came to the nursing tent seeking first aid treatment.

The reporter told how Nola Forrest and Edna Traeger had planned their exhibit to show the complete wardrobe issued to Army nurses by the Quartermaster Corps plus the field pieces used in combat duty — steel helmets, canteens, and gas masks. On display were numerous posters, photographs of nurses at work, and plenty of printed handouts telling the Army Nurse Corps story.

Nola said she and Edna handed out "pounds and pounds of literature" to teenage girls and others who were intrigued by the idea of joining the Army Nurse Corps. To be accepted they had to have a high school diploma, certification of graduation from an accredited school for nurses, certification as a registered nurse, and be a U.S. citizen. Applicants were required to be between the ages of 22 and 30 years (or 21 and 40 for reserve nurses).

They received $90 a month plus quarters and subsistence (room and board) and were entitled to medical care, sick leave, hospitalization, paid vacation leave, retirement with pay, and government life insurance.

At that time Army nurses were required to be single. On September 30, 1942, however, the rules changed, and nurses on active duty who married were allowed to remain in the Corps but were still required to serve for the duration.

Nola and Edna were in the show's Exhibit Area from 2:00 p.m. until the show was over at eleven. Unlike the men in Tent City, the nurses were quartered in hotels. Nola remembered the Hotel Sherman in Chicago and declared, "I know how an actress feels to come in at midnight and order a big dinner sent up." She spent her mornings visiting local hospitals in whatever city the show had encamped and "giving a little pitch for the Army Nurse Corps." She also visited with the local Red Cross recruitment committees and made sure that any affiliated hospital units that were filling their nursing quotas were mentioned in the local papers. The Army Nurse Corps had set a goal of twenty-five hundred new members a month.

Cleveland was the next stop after Chicago, and it proved to be the last for this tour. "I remember that," Nola stated, "because Edna and I were out to Mrs. Bolton's home for lunch when we were there. I had known her a little through the office because she was very friendly and helped with the Army Nurse Corps a lot."

Nola was referring to the help Rep. Frances Payne Bolton of Ohio had given the Corps by sponsoring measures to provide almost $5 million to assist schools of nursing and graduate nursing students. In 1943 she would sponsor another bill creating the U.S. Cadet Nurse Corps, and later would introduce a bill to provide full military rank for Army nurses.

"In less than three months," Nola recalled, "the nurse that had been relieving me got sick, and so I had to go back to the office. The night I left the show was from Cleveland ... and I had this peculiar feeling. We were going on the train back to Washington, and we were leaving at midnight. I said to Blevins Davis, 'You know, I think we're going to have a wreck on this train.'

"Well, we got on the train, and I still had this feeling. I undressed and got in my berth, and at 2:00 a.m. I got up and put my clothes on because I still had this premonition. And at seven o'clock the train stopped. I thought, oh, here it is! Then it started up again, but just at that moment the crash came. The other train plowed right into us. It hit us from the back and killed the switchman and about fifteen people in our train and knocked me out."

When Nola revived, a man said he was glad she was talking. She told him, "We're nurses, and we'll see what we can do." Then she noticed Edna's berth was empty and she found her in the dressing room sitting on a chair. The mirror had crashed on her head, and "she was just kind of smiling, and she said, 'What happened?' So I told her, and she quickly went out [and started to help].

"The conductor came, and he said, 'My God, there's people back here dead and dying.' In the dining car the forks had just stuck right into the wall, like this. And in the train that was next, the car was burning. There was a person that was on fire on top of the car. I said to ask the conductor if there was a doctor, if he didn't have a first aid kit. It had been raining, and we took blankets out and put them on the ground, and they carried people out.

"This one man said he was a doctor, I don't know if he was, but he'd ask me [questions]. Then they came and said there was this ensign who was trapped in a car in the other train, and he was hurt very badly, and they wanted to give him a big dose of morphine, which I had to fix. I think the poor fellow died."

The accident happened at 7:35 on the morning of September 24, 1942. The Cleveland night express to Washington stopped to repair an engine and had just started up again when the Detroit-to-Baltimore Ambassador plowed into the rear of the Cleveland train. The impact tossed the rear sleeper onto an adjoining track where it was struck by a fast, westbound freight train. The three trains were piled up in a narrow cut at Dickerson, Maryland, a "scene of utter chaos, littered with over-turned and derailed cars … crackling flames of burning cars … agonized screams of the injured and dying," according to a news account.

After a while, a relief train came along and carried the nurses to Silver Spring, Maryland. One paper lauded the heroism of "the two WAACs," which provided a laugh for the participants. *The Washington Post* got the story straight. Its reporter noted that a Coast Guard captain, an Army doctor, and two Army nurses, all of whom were passengers, org-anized the rescue before local hospitals and Red Cross units arrived on the scene. At final count, fourteen people lost their lives in the disaster.

"We got off at Walter Reed," Nola recalled, "because I had this arm that was all black and blue where I'd hit something. I wasn't really hurt." Right away, she was back in the surgeon general's office as head of nurs-ing personnel.

CHAPTER 4

# TRIAL RUN

I n December 1942 a new law provided relative rank for all members of the Army and Navy Nurse Corps with the same pay and allowances as officers of comparable rank in other branches of the service. Congress had recently authorized pay equal to that of military men for women from civilian life who joined the Army Auxiliary Corps and the Navy, Coast Guard, and Marine Reserves and could scarcely do less for nurses who were already on the military payroll.

Better pay might help Captain Forrest and her colleagues in their recruitment task. But back in her post as chief of nursing personnel, Nola's heart was still set on foreign duty. That may have been why she suddenly found herself in a new and demanding environment that in many ways resembled a foreign theater.

"They came in and said that they had to set up a theater of operations out in the desert," she explained. "They called it the Desert Training Center. It was expected to be operated exactly as [an active theater]. You had your first aid station, and you had your field hospital and then your station hospital and the general hospital. This was more than two hundred thousand acres of land. The distances were very great. It went down as far as Yuma, Arizona, and [up to] Needles, California, every hot place in the world. General Patton had his group there first. They said he used to tell his soldiers after they got to Africa, if they didn't behave, he'd send them back to the desert."

In March 1943 when Nola arrived as director of nurses, the Center had expanded from a limited experiment to a full military training complex. The concept had originated earlier that year when the United States entered the world conflict and military leaders found themselves confronted with the demands of global warfare. German forces under Field Marshal Erwin Rommel were driving the British toward Egypt in the sand and blistering heat. The Japanese in the high mountains of Indochina were moving toward Burma, and the Soviets were battling the Germans in a frozen swamp near Novgorod.

The U.S. War Department could foresee battles engaging American soldiers in harsh terrain — hot sand, dense jungle, rocky cliffs, and icy ground. Conditions would call for new techniques of fighting, new ways to use weapons and equipment, and new methods of supply and communication. Human bodies needed the strength to withstand extreme changes in climate and the threat of dehydration.

In March 1942 the Army sent Gen. George S. Patton, Jr. to reconnoiter a training site in southeastern California and western Arizona. He discovered a desolate wasteland, served by three railroads and crossed by three highways. Virtually no one lived there. On the perimeter were three small towns — Needles and Blyth on the eastern border of California, and Yuma on the edge of neighboring Arizona. A fourth town, Indio, was located in California twenty-five miles to the west of the desert center.

Patton was delighted with what he found. The entire area, which comprised the Sonora Desert and further acreage to the north and south, was about the size of Vermont and New Hampshire combined. According to one writer, "There were sandy stretches, rocks, crags, dry salt-lake beds, mountains, precipitous gorges—a varied terrain with little shade and sparse vegetation. Sudden changes in weather sent temperatures climbing from below freezing during the night to over 100 degrees the next day. Sandstorms and cloudbursts were frequent occurrences."

For the base camp of his I Armored Corps, Patton chose a site twenty miles east of Indio. For his men he set up three other divisional centers in scattered areas in the desert. He decided that the soldiers would live in tents without electric lights, sheets, heat, or hot water. The administration buildings would be made of plain wood covered with tar paper.

Patton had fewer than ten thousand officers and enlisted men in his experimental training program, which was not to exceed six weeks. His plan was to build teamwork between members of armored units and between air and ground units, moving in stages from smaller to larger groups. The culmination of the training would be a combined field exercise lasting several days, moving troops three hundred miles through the desert, provisioned by advanced bases of supply. The men would fire service ammunition, and combat aviation would drop live bombs.

Here Patton evolved the tactics he would later use in overseas campaigns. He required all his men to be able to run a mile in ten minutes with full field pack and rifles. Within a month all the men were able to do so. The general took part in the exercises, and from a hill known as The King's Throne he shouted instructions and commands into his radio.

By the end of July 1942, Patton and his I Armored Corps left the desert training ground to prepare for a landing in Casablanca the following November. Back at the training center, two new commands were brought in and encountered confusion with no administrative link between them. The full ingredients of virtual war — all types of units, combat and service, under combat conditions — were still missing. The concept of the Desert Training Center (DTC) was then broadened, and by the early months of 1943 the Center was ready to function as a full-scale theater, the first in the United States.

Combat units and service groups began to arrive in force. In February and March two armored divisions, a motorized division, a tank group, a mechanized cavalry group, two tank destroyer battalions, and a coast artillery battalion for antiaircraft defense were engaged in maneuvers. An array of support services backed them up. These included supply and transportation plus a series of medical units — from aid stations to field, evacuation, and base hospitals.

When Capt. Nola Forrest took up her duties, the Center was in ferment. She was assigned to the 20th Headquarters, Medical Service in Banning, California, in the Communications Zone. Her office was located some thirty miles northwest of the Center headquarters in the Combat Zone. She found the medical system straining to provide care for a population of more than ninety thousand. New buildings were rising everywhere, and military units of every description were moving back and forth across the vast expanse of the training grounds.

Two days after she came, Nola was promoted to the relative rank of major in the Army Nurse Corps with base pay of $3,000 a year, plus subsistence and quarters. Brig. Gen. Norman T. Kirk, her associate from Manila days, about to become the new surgeon general of the Army, came out to inspect the Center and pinned the oak leaf insignia on her shoulders.

Nola chose Edna Traeger, soon to become a captain, as her assistant. Their headquarters was located on a highway over which they had to travel many miles through hot, arid country to various points in the desert for inspection trips. Their mission was to check on the type and quality of the nursing service, as well as on the living conditions, recreation, training, and morale of the nurses, all of whom were being prepared for rigorous overseas duty.

Nola made an initial report, dated April 8, 1943, to Col. Florence Blanchfield, acting superintendent of the Army Nurse Corps. She described fewer than 250 nurses working in ten medical centers in small towns, in two centers in Camp Young, and at the headquarters of the Communications Zone in Banning. Most of the medical units were station hospitals. The first general hospital would open in Spadra, California, in May with a bed capacity of one thousand.

Medical management was in a state of flux with hospitals waiting either for equipment, for nurses, or to be moved to new quarters. Some units were in tents, and some were in buildings. Some nurses had engaged in field maneuvers and were established in their duties. Others were newly arrived and restless to start working.

"The scope and magnitude of the operations in the Desert Training Center are amazing and unimaginable," Nola reported. "There are many difficulties and hardships that the nurses are encountering and will continue to meet. However, it is felt very strongly that the great value they will derive from this type of life and training will so overcompensate for the difficulties that there will be no comparison [with other types of training]."

A new commanding general took over the administration of the theater. Its population swelled to one hundred and ninety thousand by mid-1943. At that point Army Ground Forces issued a directive calling for more realistic conditions to harden the troops. No more perishable food was served, no concrete floors installed for showers, and screens were removed from kitchens that were used for short periods of time. The delivery of ice was stopped, and all troops subsisted on field rations except for patients in hospitals.

Soldiers were issued individual weapons, which they used under simulated combat conditions. They trained in rough-and-tumble fighting that called for extreme exertion over short periods. They heard the sounds of bursting shells close by and the crack of small arms bullets overhead. Soldiers in combat units laid mines, and every man learned how to detect and remove them. Every noncommissioned officer was trained to lead a patrol over unknown terrain at night and to infiltrate hostile positions with one group pitted against another.

Under this excessive regimen many soldiers collapsed with injuries or severe reactions to the climate. "We had a terrific heat problem," Nola recalled with sympathy, "so much so that they had to bring in these big buses that were refrigerated to put the patients in. They went almost crazy — 'crazy with the heat' was really true." Many men died from heat stroke.

The hospitals were crowded, and Nola was soon dealing with one problem after another. Her later reports, directed to the commanding general in the Communications Zone, covered the need for floored tents, the quality of the food, the need for more nurses, the condition of their quarters, and the accuracy of narcotic records. She also described the condition of showers and laundries, shortages of seersucker uniforms and coveralls, field training of nurses, their need for helmets, and low morale in some hospital units.

A letter, dated August 2, 1943, from the chief nurse at the 39th Station Hospital in Yuma gave a firsthand account:

> The terrific heat we had had day and night has made us all look like a bunch of drooping lilies. The cases of heat exhaustion, heat strokes and the meningitis cases have really put our nursing ability to a test. The heat cases require more nursing care, so the girls have worked in shifts of three hours each during the night. The patients arrive with temperatures of 108 to 110 and treatment must be started at once … They

are so violent and half-crazed, that it sometimes takes as many as five corpsmen to hold them in bed. The mortuary in Yuma is full to capacity … Some of the cases arrive dead and others die within the hour … It pleases me very much that not once have I ever heard one [nurse] gripe about working overtime. Everyone have [sic] volunteered their services, and I haven't had to request any of them to go on duty.

At the 32nd Evacuation Hospital at Horn, near Yuma, six nurses were incapacitated with heat exhaustion, and those in other hospitals showed signs of depleted energy. Nola wrote a memo to the chief surgeon of the Center, suggesting a rest camp in the mountains for tired nurses who had been in the theater many months.

That summer she forwarded an urgent memo to the surgeon general's office in Washington, pointing out that orders to the quartermaster to stock herringbone twill clothing, women's field shoes, women's leggings, and blue cotton crepe uniforms at the San Bernardino Depot had not been fulfilled. Instead, the depot was planning to send overcoats and suits. As she pointed out, these were "absolutely useless and superfluous in the desert … with its almost unbearable heat, primitive living conditions and isolation … a grueling test for 500 nurses … If this field clothing cannot be provided … it will be a great factor in the lowering of morale."

"You see, everybody lived in tents," Nola explained. "I was up at one field hospital, and it was so hot the girl showed me how she could fry an egg on a rock right outside her tent." After a day in the sun, the insides of the tents were at oven temperatures. Although some of the nurses could gain relief in hospitals where cooling systems were functioning, many had to endure oppressive heat around the clock.

And some were tormented with a plague of crickets. "Down around Yuma they had [such] a cricket infestation that the crickets would eat all the nylon," said Nola. "They'd eat the nightgowns off of the nurses almost. They'd have to keep their hose — they didn't wear hose all the time but when they did, had to keep them in glass jars."

The director and her assistant did not live in tents, but their quarters were far from lavish. "The headquarters took over a motel in Banning," Nola remembered, "and we had those cottages — no air conditioning, of course. It wasn't a very nice motel at that. It had those little wooden shacks but with a central meeting place, and they used that for a mess hall. Every morning when we went out, we would put a pitcher of water in the refrigerator to drink before dinner when we came back. I had a staff car and a driver, and I had to make all these inspection trips all over the desert, but there was never any air conditioning in the car. Most of the time you had to go at night."

Inspection trips continued throughout the summer months. Nola recalled a typical scene: "We'd traveled most of the night going over to Needles, California. We had two station hospitals there, and we had a few hospitals around. I hadn't been over there for two or three months anyhow, but there was a woman who kept a rooming house, or whatever, Mrs. Kelly. You know, hotel rooms were very hard to get in those days, but I had a contact with her. I would call her, and I would say, 'Mrs. Kelly, I'm going to get in there about three o'clock [in the morning]. Could you have a room?' 'Oh, yes, I'll have it. Just pound on the door, and somebody'll open it for you.'

"There were always two of us. Edna and I would go up to our room, and there would probably be a soldier's uniform hanging in the closet. A sorry looking place, but we always took a packet of newspapers with us, and we just put newspapers on everything, on the top of the dresser, on the top of the chair, the floor. The sheets were usually pretty clean, and that was all we had to do. And it was so hot! Of course, there was no air conditioning there either."

As time went on, the general hospital at Spadra, California, came into operation, and many more station hospitals plus field hospitals and evacuation hospitals were added throughout the area. Everywhere medical services were heavily taxed, and the harsh conditions of desert life were taking their toll on soldiers and caregivers.

Nurses could suffer in other ways than heat depletion. One of them came to Nola and confessed, "I'm pregnant, and I don't know what to do." A medical officer had invited her for a ride in a jeep to see the sunset, driven a distance, then parked and said, "Come across." He raped her, but she told no one — what would people think of her? When she confided in Nola, she heard her say, "You know what I have to do. I have no choice but to discharge you."

The director was not in a position to plead the nurse's case. The nurse herself would have to bring a charge of rape against a male officer who probably outranked her. She would have been required to testify before a military board of inquiry made up entirely of officers, all men. They would have been reluctant to impose a heavy punishment on a peer. The nurse's pregnancy would also have been revealed with damage to her future career.

This one subsequently underwent a botched abortion in Los Angeles where Nola visited her as she was recovering in a private hospital. Later, when the nurse was offered an administrative position in a state medical facility in the East, she got in touch to find out if the incident was on her record. She learned that the Army Nurse Corps did not leave such a stigma in the files of its members. Colonel Blanchfield had ruled that the records of nurses discharged for pregnancy carry a diagnosis of "cyesis," an obsolete medical term.

Some nurses in the Center encountered other dangers. Those who worked in field hospitals underwent a month-long infiltration course simulating the hazards and hardships of actual warfare. They took 20-mile hikes with full field packs in suffocating temperatures, and they climbed rope ladders over steep barriers. They crawled on the ground under barbed wire with live bullets flying thirty-six inches above their heads. To allay their fears, Nola took that part of the course herself and found the test an ordeal.

In July she announced with pride at a press conference that one nurse held the record for crawling seventy-five yards in seven minutes under fire. Her time beat all the men, much to their chagrin. *The New York Times* ran a headline, "Weaker Sex Theory Disproved in Desert."

Two nurses met special challenges that made the news. Second Lieutenant Edith Greenwood was the first woman to receive the Soldier's Medal for rescuing fifteen bed patients from a burning hospital, and 2nd Lt. Margaret Decker received the same award for saving a soldier from drowning in the Colorado River. This medal is given for acts of heroism not involving conflict with an armed enemy but involving personal hazard and the voluntary risk of life.

To ease the pressures of training, the troops sought escape on the edges of the theater where the small communities were deluged with visitors. The original training camp was only twenty-five miles from Indio, California. The town consisted of fifteen hundred people, a small hotel, a movie theater, and a few restaurants and stores. Almost overnight nine thousand soldiers rushed into the streets on buses. Thirsty GIs might easily wait more than one hour in line for a coke or stand eight deep for restaurant seats. Telephone service broke down. The Army mess officers bought meat and vegetables locally, virtually cleaning out the grocery shelves.

In Indio, despite the drain on their facilities, most of the townspeople were friendly to the soldiers, offered hospitality, organized recreation, and brought in a USO (United Service Organizations) club for dances. Commercial entertainment expanded in the form of bars, pool halls, and hot dog stands.

As the Center expanded, soldiers poured into Yuma and Banning. They were followed by their girlfriends and wives, many with children. Family members lived in trailers, one-room cabins, shacks, garages, and tents. Sometimes a bed served three different occupants in a 24-hour period. Wives became waitresses, sales clerks, and typists, helping to meet the overload from booming business.

Nola would take a weekend off once in a while to get away from the relentless heat, traveling to Los Angeles by train. In August she even took a 10-day leave. She stayed in the Beverly Hills Hotel with a friend. When they went to the Brown Derby for a meal, a long line of people were usually waiting for a table, but the Army Nurse Corps uniform got her party in ahead of the others.

On one return trip actor Nelson Eddy, known to millions of moviegoers, walked back in the train and introduced himself to Nola. He and his wife Ann invited her to dinner in the dining car to discuss the singer's interest in giving a concert for the troops. He was like many other entertainers — singers, comedians, actors, and musicians — who offered their talents to raise the morale of the men in service.

At the Center Leopold Stokowski conducted one hundred musicians in Shostakovich's *Leningrad Symphony*; famed soprano Jane Winterly sang, and musical comedian Victor Borge held the stage with his "phonetic punctuation." The Army tried to provide relief from the constant pressure by establishing a nighttime baseball league and adding post exchanges and day rooms.

These diversions and amenities were fleetingly enjoyed as troops moved in, were trained, and moved on. Hospital staffs were moving as well. One example of the endless shifting among medical units was the departure in September of the 13th General Hospital from Spadra to prepare for embarkation for New Guinea in January 1944. This affiliate from the Presbyterian Hospital in Chicago, Illinois, was replaced by the Army's 34th General Hospital — a typical exchange.

Toward the end of 1943 operations in the desert were diminishing in scale because of the smaller number of troop divisions and air units remaining in the States and the lack of service units, which were rapidly shipping overseas. Recommendations were made at the highest Army levels to close the California-Arizona Maneuver Area (C-AMA), as it was then called, and the following spring all training operations ceased.

Meanwhile Major Forrest received orders on December 11, 1943 to report to Washington, D.C. She had already briefed the C-AMA surgeon in the Communications Zone on the nursing activities from March through November of that year. Her summary stated that 685 nurses were then serving in twenty installations in the area. During the March-to-November period, she had managed the nursing staffs of thirty-six hospitals in the training center: five field hospitals, ten evacuation hospitals, seventeen station hospitals, and four general hospitals, three of which had gone into operation in the previous three months.

She had had responsibility for the welfare of almost twelve hundred nurses. She stated that "many nurses had gone to overseas stations from the desert, grateful for the experiences they had gained ... Here they learned to make the physical adjustments so necessary for their life on foreign duty."

In January 1, 1944 she reported to Colonel Blanchfield on her visits to eleven nursing facilities at ports of embarkation on the West Coast where nurses were in staging areas, waiting for deployment to stations overseas or to hospital ships. She described the management at each location — including the supply or deficiency of uniforms. By this time the Army quartermaster had agreed to manufacture slacks for nurses, but their delivery to overseas theaters was another question.

Nola was returning to her former job in Washington, D.C., yet she did not feel that her grueling tour in the desert had earned her the right to remain on home duty. She kept alive her request for an overseas transfer. That fall Colonel Blanchfield had complimented her in a letter on the "very efficient administration of the nursing service from your office" and added that she did not have to be reminded of Nola's wish for an overseas posting, stating that "... we are constantly watching for an assignment commensurate with your grade or a higher grade."

CHAPTER 5

# DOWN UNDER

In January 1944, Nola Forrest replaced Lt. Col. Ida Danielson, who had taken her place and was about to be transferred to London. A few months earlier Ida had scrawled at the bottom of an official letter, "What about coming back to the office?"

In ANC headquarters the returning head of personnel looked out from her desk on a turbulent scene. Inquiries and applications streamed in by the hundreds. Chief nurses wrote or dropped by with problems of housing, feeding, and morale. Telephones rang constantly. Questions regarding transportation, uniforms, and Army customs called for answers. Speeches and articles were in preparation, and interviews awaited scheduling. A huge file in one corner of the office, showing the location of every nurse in the service, had to be updated as each nurse was accepted, assigned, or transferred.

Thousands of Army nurses were on active duty at home and abroad, and more were needed. American newspapers and magazines lauded the heroism of nurses who were tending the wounded around the world, and the movie industry used its stars to tell their story. A film entitled *So Proudly We Hail*, featuring Claudette Colbert, Paulette Goddard, Veronica Lake, and Barbara Britton, dramatized the courage of the Army and Navy nurses who had cared for hundreds of U.S. troops trapped on Bataan and Corregidor at the outbreak of the war in the Philippines.

The moviemakers effectively recreated their jungle background, hospital facilities and clothing, but the film's false and misleading portrayals and romanticized story line offended the nurses who had endured the real conditions. A second version of their ordeal, *Cry Havoc*, starring Margaret Sullavan, Ann Sothern, Joan Blondell, and Fay Bainter, was harsher. In any case, both movies were hugely popular with the general public as showcases for military nurses in action.

In February 1944 six Army nurses were killed in Italy during bombing attacks on the Anzio beachhead. At month's end Nola Forrest was promoted to the relative rank of lieutenant colonel in the Army Nurse Corps, one of twenty-six nurses to reach this level. She was now in a position to assume greater responsibility, perhaps a dangerous overseas assignment.

In her field tours she had demonstrated her public relations skills, her sound judgment, and the clarity and accuracy of her reports. She was familiar with the issues involved in dealing with staff members on various levels of the Medical Department. She was determined to assume the risks of serving in a combat theater. In fact, she relished the prospect.

"Then," said Nola, "they decided they were going to bring back the nurse who had been director of nurses out in the Southwest Pacific. She was quite a bit older than the rest of us, and it had been a little difficult for her." This nurse was Lt. Col. Martha Jane Clement, who had been chief nurse of the station hospital at Fort Mills on the island of Corregidor when Nola was assigned to Sternberg General Hospital in Manila in the late 1920s.

Colonel Clement was one of the first American nurses to reach Australia at the start of the war. Only a few hundred others had preceded her when she arrived by ship in April 1942 after a rough voyage. Two years later she was known to thousands of U.S. soldiers in the Southwest Pacific as "Ma" Clement. According to an article in the September 1944 issue of *Cosmopolitan* magazine, this large, energetic woman had endeared herself to anxious, bedridden soldiers for her empathy and her camaraderie. Now fifty-six years of age, she was recalled from foreign duty as new policies placed the overseas age limit at forty-five.

"I spoke up," Nola continued, "and finally talked them into letting me go out there," even though she herself would turn forty-four in June.

Arrangements had to be made, and not until June 26th was a telegram sent to GHQ SWPA (General Headquarters, Southwest Pacific Area), stating that Lt. Col. Nola Forrest was assigned to that command as a replacement for Lt. Col. Martha Clement.

By this time Nola's rank was no longer relative. In June 1944, the 78th Congress passed Public Law 350, granting nurses temporary commissions in the U.S. Army with full pay and privileges for the grades from second lieutenant through colonel for the duration plus six months.

After two weeks' leave with pay Nola was glad to receive orders from the adjutant general's office assigning her to "permanent station outside continental U.S., tropical climate, to be available after July 20, 1944." She was authorized "... 2 pr trousers, HBT [herringbone twill]; 2 ea. shirts, HBT; 2 pr leggings, canvas; 2 pr shoes, field; 4 pr anklets, wool; canteens, aluminum, plastic or stainless steel and a trunk locker."

On July 25th she left Washington, and soon a photo in the *Chicago Tribune* showed her seated at the Hotel Sherman with Colonel Clement, other nurses, and a Red Cross committee woman. She was reported as "en route to a new assignment that she hopes will take her overseas." A mention was also made of Colonel Clement's posting as chief nurse in the Army's 6th service command in Chicago.

A few days later Nola Forrest arrived in San Francisco to await available transportation. The Army quartermaster issued her forty-three items, including a sweater and an overcoat for the winter in Australia, plus Arctic overshoes despite the fact that she would arrive in the antipodal springtime. "I was ordered there," she recalled, "and I went to the Canterbury Hotel where I had stayed before, and had to go down to Fort Mason every morning. 'Just report tomorrow morning,' they'd say, and so I'd report. Then one day they said, 'You come on board at six o'clock tonight.'"

That day was the fifth of August. "I went down to the ship, and I was the only nurse because I was a replacement. There were about twenty Red Cross women and, I think, a physical therapist and a dietitian. We went to bed, and when we woke up in the morning, we were out through the Golden Gate.

"The ship was the old *Republic* I had come back on from Manila [formerly the USS *U. S. Grant*]. There were three or four of us in my cabin. We had to get up about four thirty in the morning at first light. General alarm sounded, and we had to put on our life jackets and stand silently on deck at our battle stations for up to an hour and a half," during the most likely time for submarine attacks. When the All Clear was heard, the passengers could return to their cabins with little time left for napping.

"We were at sea for almost a month," as Nola remembered. "There was nothing to do, of course." Still she managed to find one way to enjoy herself. "You were completely blacked out at night," she said, "with no light on deck at all. The doors even were blacked out — you had to throw big blankets over them. But I'll tell you what I did. There was a poker game going on, Red Dog. I think the dietitian and I were the only two women [included], but it was the captain of the ship and the colonel of the troops and the chaplain. There were about six of us, and we usually played every night. Of course, you couldn't have any money. On a ship you can't gamble. You can't have any liquor either. We used match books."

Their debarkation was delayed for several days. "We were supposed to land in Brisbane," Nola went on. "Well, fighting had been going on [in some of the islands] at that time, and the ship was diverted, and we landed at Finschhafen up in New Guinea. A chief nurse there and General [Frane] Baker, who was in command of that area, met me, and I stayed in the quarters all night.

"The next morning they had a plane to Townsville [Australia], and I spent the night there. Then the next day came and another flight on a bucket seat took me into Brisbane." These were long flights — some eight hundred miles south from Finschhafen to Townsville and another seven hundred miles from Townsville down to Brisbane.

Nola's new post was in an industrial city at about the midpoint of Australia's east coast. Settled in 1824 as a penal colony, Brisbane soon became self-supporting through land reclamation and immigration, and by the 20th century was a flourishing urban center with a university, an art gallery, and a museum. It had been chosen by MacArthur as the headquarters of the Southwest Pacific Area (SWPA) command.

Upon her arrival, Nola was met by Brig. Gen. Guy B. Denit, chief medical officer, and Maj. Pauline Kirby, who had been assistant to "Ma" Clement and would be Nola's assistant from now on. They took her to

Lennon's Hotel, "which was a very nice, plush place to live." Only American generals and full colonels were billeted there, but as the ranking woman officer in the theater, the SWPA director of nurses was billeted there, too. As soon as she settled in, the chief nurse of the Australian nurse corps, who was addressed as *Sister*, came to pay her an official visit.

On September 1, 1944, Nola Forrest reported for duty. Her orders assigned her to Headquarters, USASOS (United States Army Services of Supply) within the SWPA command. Almost immediately she began inspection trips to the remaining U.S. Army hospitals dispersed throughout the eastern half of the continent.

Months before, the tide of battle had turned to the offensive for the Allies. As part of a broader campaign to retake the Philippines General MacArthur had started two years earlier moving his troops along the northeastern coast of New Guinea, using a leapfrog strategy, sometimes bypassing enemy areas. By the end of July 1944 he had captured Sansapor two thousand miles away at the far end of the Vogelkop peninsula, closing out the New Guinea campaign.

Australia served as a huge supply base for military operations to the north. As occupied areas became secure, Army support services, including hospitals and medical staff, arrived as fast as engineers could prepare the ground for construction and transport was available. In the first two or three months of the New Guinea warfare, sick and wounded Allied soldiers were evacuated by ship for treatment on the continent, but as early as October 1942, hospitals and nurses arrived in Port Moresby on the southwestern coast of the island. As fighting advanced, other hospitals were erected closer to combat areas, eliminating the need for shipment south.

By the time Nola reached the theater, most U.S. Army hospitals were already in New Guinea. In the spring of 1944 a large number of general and station hospitals were staged at Milne Bay, waiting to move on. By summer the big 4th General Hospital in Melbourne had moved to Finschhafen, and other hospitals were moving north having transferred their local patients to Australian hospitals or the U.S. Navy. Even so, Nola recalled, "We had lots of hospitals. We had a chief nurse in Melbourne, another one in Sydney. Then we had Townsville. I had to go and see them all."

General Denit told her right away, "You are in charge of the nurses. Do what you think is best, and I will back you up." Her role as advisor to Denit, chief surgeon, USASOS (and also chief surgeon of the theater), was to assist in formulating policies for the ANC and to inspect all installations in regard to the quality of nursing service, living conditions, training, and morale. She was to visit hospitals, hospital ships, dispensaries, and rest areas.

This meant flying back and forth over great distances around the east coast of Australia as well as to hospitals inland. Returning from "doing her rounds" Nola relished her life in Brisbane. An inspection trip could last two or three days; then she would come back, spent and weary, to her home base.

"I could have fought the war at Lennon's Hotel," she remarked. "This was a place that you could call in the morning and your breakfast would be sent up with fresh pineapple. Then if you wanted to entertain, you'd come home from the office, and your furniture would be moved out of your room and a table would be put in, and you had your dinner served. You went to the movies, came home, and your bed was back in your room. It was plush. And wonderful, wonderful food! The reason you didn't eat in the dining room was because we were on the [austerity] economy and you had to eat what the dining room served if you went in there.

"General MacArthur had, I think, the whole sixth floor — General and Mrs. MacArthur and little Arthur and the amah [nursemaid]. I saw her, and I saw him quite often, coming in and out of the hotel or out of the building where our offices were. But I don't think anyone ever knew him too well. He was devoted to his wife and devoted to his child. He came home at noon, and then he stayed home until about four o'clock and went back to the office until eight or nine. So she was alone a lot of the time, and as I was the only other woman in the hotel, she'd sometimes ask me to come up. She was charming."

Jean MacArthur had been living in Lennon's Hotel since July 1942 when her husband moved his headquarters to Brisbane. That was a desperate time for the general and all those under his command. As the year began, the Australian government, fearing invasion, had demanded the return of three of their divisions fighting in North Africa since the start of the war. When Great Britain's Prime Minister Winston Churchill refused, the Australians agreed to moderate their demand if the Allies would send an American general with American troops to follow.

A decision was then made at the highest levels to give MacArthur that command and to build a base on the continent for assemblage of troops, aircraft, and supplies for the start of an offensive against Japan. In February 1942, President Roosevelt ordered MacArthur to Australia while the general and his diseased and half-starved troops were under siege on Bataan and Corregidor. The general's first impulse was to resist abandoning his embattled men to their certain capture, feeling morally bound to share their fate. Then, moved by the strong protests of his staff, he agreed to go but delayed his departure.

Further cables from Washington and growing signs of Japanese awareness brought action. On March 11th he set out under cover of darkness with his family and a few officers in four fragile PT boats. The party, running through a minefield and dodging Japanese lookouts, reached Mindanao halfway to their destination two days later while the island was under attack but still under U.S. control.

There they waited anxiously several days for two worn-out B-17s to come and fly them to Australia. Eluding Japanese fighter planes most of the way, the pilots managed to reach the continent on March 17th. They were headed for Darwin on the north coast, but the planes were diverted to Batchelor Field forty miles to the south when radio intercepts warned of a Japanese attack. Still fleeing before enemy pursuers, the group was flown to Alice Springs and then traveled on by rail.

The Australians had reason to fear further attacks. The Japanese perimeter extended five thousand miles from Tokyo in almost all directions. Japanese forces held the Philippines, Singapore, Hong Kong, the Dutch East Indies, Malaya, the Bismarck islands, the Gilberts, Timor, Wake, Guam, Borneo, the northern Solomons, and the western half of New Guinea. They had struck at Darwin on February 19th, sinking seventeen ships in the harbor and downing twenty-two Allied planes as well as destroying many private homes.

On March 21st, MacArthur arrived in Melbourne on the southeastern tip of the continent where he was greeted by boisterous crowds.

A few days later in Canberra, the capital, he told Australian leaders he doubted the Japanese were well enough equipped to mount an invasion of their country. He knew, however, that he was facing overwhelming odds.

The moment he stepped off the plane at Batchelor Field he learned that there were only twenty-five thousand American troops in Australia, mostly airmen and engineers. Most Australian troops and air force units were still in North Africa or the Middle East, and most of the combat strength of the Australian navy was in the Mediterranean. MacArthur was also painfully aware of the decision made by Roosevelt and Churchill to put victory over Germany ahead of victory over Japan.

In April the President named him commander in chief of the Southwest Pacific Area (CINCSOWESPAC). This territory encompassed Australia, the Solomon Islands, the Bismarck Archipelago, New Guinea, the Netherlands East Indies (except Sumatra), and the Philippines. His command would chiefly employ land- and air-based troops. Admiral Chester W. Nimitz, usually referred to as CINCPAC, was given a territory ranging from Alaska to the Antarctic, known as Pacific Ocean Areas (POA), divided into three theaters. He commanded a vast fleet of naval ships and air forces.

Right after MacArthur's appointment to the SWPA command the Japanese sent troop ships and escorting carriers from the island of Guadalcanal toward southern New Guinea as part of their plan to take Port Moresby by sea. American naval intelligence deciphered their messages, and two U.S. naval carrier task forces rushed to intercept the enemy.

The ensuing Battle of the Coral Sea lasted five days in May 1942 and made naval history. Fought in waters between the eastern end of Papua and the northeast coast of Australia five hundred miles away, it was the first to be waged by an exchange of air strikes launched from aircraft carriers. No opposing warships directly fired upon or even sighted each other. The U.S. Navy lost the carrier *Lexington* and suffered severe damage to the *Yorktown*, but the Allies gained a strategic victory by halting the Japanese southward expansion.

With the threat of invasion lifted and after a crucial American victory at Midway in June, MacArthur prepared to take the offensive. His forces had been augmented by the return of two Australian infantry divisions and nearly one hundred thousand American troops. Part of the Allied operations plan was to seize the northeastern coast of New Guinea. The first move was the development of an airfield near Buna, the site of an Australian government mission.

The Japanese landed there first to form a beachhead for a thrust to take Port Moresby from behind. After losing four aircraft carriers at Midway, they planned to advance overland this time. Soon five thousand enemy soldiers and mules were pushing themselves and their heavy artillery up the steep precipices of the Owen Stanley Range toward the port.

On July 22nd, Australian soldiers engaged the Japanese for the first time in the thickets and swamps of the mountain jungle and in a few weeks were joined by American reinforcements. Soldiers on both sides experienced enervating heat and humidity on the shoreline and biting cold and drenching rain halfway up the mountainsides. The sawtoothed jungle range rose as high as thirteen thousand feet. The men had to hack their way through kunai grass that grew seven feet high. The ground was slippery, their packs and weapons were heavy, and leeches and mosquitoes bit into human flesh.

They were attacked by diseases that included malaria and dengue fever. They were threatened with scrub typhus, which could bring death. They suffered from tormenting fungal skin eruptions, known as "jungle rot." They were hungry. Their feet swelled. And almost all of them were weakened with dysentery. Hospital corpsmen carried the sick and wounded through jungles to clearing stations without a letup.

That summer Allied soldiers in New Guinea met the enemy in another engagement. As one prong of a counterattack MacArthur assembled troops and engineers at Milne Bay, at the easternmost tip of the island. Here the Allies had two airfields, and late in August the Japanese mounted an assault on their position. But defending troops, aided by fighter pilots, smashed their effort, marking the first major Allied ground victory in the Pacific war.

In September the Japanese were closing in on Port Moresby thirty miles from their line of advance. At this point, though, they were severely weakened by disease and starvation. Their soldiers were eating grass and leaves and dying from malaria, dysentery, and enteritis. At the end of the month Imperial Headquarters decided to retrench and moved the exhausted troops back over the mountains toward Buna and

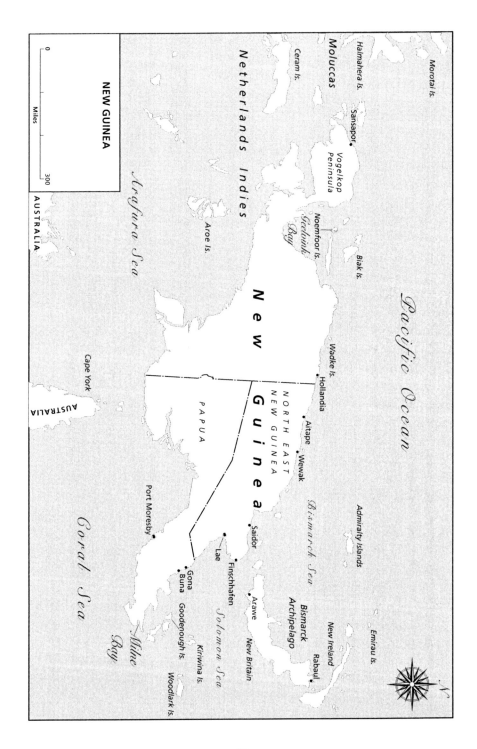

NEW GUINEA

0     Miles     300

AUSTRALIA

Gona to serve as reinforcements for their forces on Guadalcanal.

Medical groups often had no way to transport sick and wounded Allied soldiers and no field hospitals to send them to. When possible, they used native litter-bearers to carry the wounded on primitive jungle trails down to the shore for shipment to the continent by sea. As the Australians pushed after the enemy, they built airfields in the mountains so that planes could fly in troops and evacuate the wounded to Port Moresby, where hospitals opened in the fall.

The first hospital to set down in New Guinea was the 153rd Station Hospital, sent to Port Moresby in October 1942. Here the working conditions resembled combat support. The stresses of duty were described in the July 1944 issue of *The American Journal of Nursing*: "Rain rushing down the tents would wash away the nurses' shoes. Night nurses were up to their knees in mud as they treated 250 to 300 patients each. Keeping the operating rooms sterile was a problem... the nurses [did what they could to bring] order out of chaos."

Two months later the 10th Evacuation Hospital and 171st Station Hospital were added to the complex. The new nurses found themselves inundated with work and, like everyone else, running for shelter from constant air raids. Medical equipment was far from adequate, and nurses used fuse boxes for sterile dressings and metal ammunition-box liners for sinks in the operating rooms. In January, an inspecting officer called their quarters "very, very poor."

Capt. Martha Jane Clement (promoted to lieutenant colonel in 1943) began to visit the New Guinea hospitals, flying over the dangerous thunderheads of the Owen Stanley Range. Famed for her motherly qualities, she saw to the welfare of the nurses and comforted wounded men in the wards. Both soldiers and nurses could ask for her key at Lennon's Hotel in Brisbane and rest and bathe in her suite even in her absence.

Port Moresby resembled a frontier town. Engineers building roads and airfields created ruts that filled with rainwater. Mosquitoes bred in stagnant pools under the sun, and malaria cases rose precipitously. All three of the town's hospitals overflowed with casualties from the Buna-Gona campaign, but in the early days even as more hospitals were added, they held more malaria cases than battle wounded.

Malaria was spread by mosquitoes that feasted on human hosts, and the relapse rate was very high. By August 1943 a special organization to fight the disease was set up within USASOS and Atabrine , a new antimalarial drug, was given shipping priority. Military teams came to conquered areas to enforce controls.

Everyone wore protective clothing. Stagnant pools were drained, vegetation sprayed, cans flattened, and mosquito nets placed over every sleeper. Soldiers in mess lines were forced at gunpoint to swallow Atabrine tablets; Tokyo Rose told them the pills would make them sterile.

Other endemic fevers as well as amebic and bacillary dysentery, tropical ulcers, and hepatitis taxed the skills of the doctors and nurses. The troops also suffered from hookworm, scrub typhus, and yaws. Many became psychiatric cases, their stamina drained from days of smothering heat and inadequate food, from lying in wet trenches, in swamps, and enduring constant fear.

As the Japanese retreated toward their base at Buna, the Allies regrouped to take the enemy stronghold in a debilitating push against jungle obstacles and Japanese tenacity. Their food rations and supplies were replenished by air drops. At the end of the year they captured the village of Gona a few miles up the coast, followed by Buna in early January 1943.

Late that month the capture of Sanananda closed the Papua campaign. It had taken six months of bitter and heroic fighting, inflicting greater losses on the Allies than on the Japanese. Sickness from heat exhaustion and myriad fevers had caused almost as many casualties as from combat

As time went on, relay teams carried the wounded from battalion aid stations to collecting stations and portable surgical hospitals where operations were often performed under enemy fire. The portable hospital, designed to handle twenty-five beds, was an innovation first used in the Buna struggle. Medical officers and corpsmen carried the component parts up and down jungle trails and assembled them under cotton tents close to fighting lines or in huts built by Papuan workers and shielded by trees and vegetation.

The portables were hugely successful in their surgical task of stabilizing men wounded in nearby combat. But soon they were so overwhelmed with malaria cases that only 10 percent of their load was made up of the injured. As the casualties were transported to fixed hospitals in Port Moresby, the treatment of fevers was a major concern of the nurses on duty.

In combat zones the Army nurses were conspicuous by their absence. Male technicians assumed their duties in mobile medical units. These men, even though they were of enlisted rank, worked under fire to perform skilled surgical tasks. Later on, friction resulted when the nurses appeared in occupied areas to reclaim their jobs and give orders. The technicians resented the fact that they were denied officer status (no male nurses could serve in the Army Nurse Corps). The nurses, in turn, felt deprived of opportunities to perform the professional work for which they had volunteered.

⊷ ▰◆▰ ⊶

When Nola Forrest assumed her new duties in the fall of 1944, nurses had been moving to Australia and from there to New Guinea for two years. The first nurse to reach the continent was 2nd Lt. Floramund Ann Fellmeth, who had escaped from Manila December 31, 1941 with a boatload of 224 seriously ill patients on the *Mactan*, a makeshift, ant-infested hospital ship. After a harrowing journey, the ship landed in Sydney late in January. Fellmeth was awarded the Legion of Merit for this and subsequent wartime service.

In February 1942, Army nurses began to come from the United States with hospital units. Capt. Mary Connell, the chief nurse of a group of twenty-five with the 5th Station Hospital, described their voyage on the USS *Panama*. They were among several hundred nurses traveling at the same time on three or four other vessels. These included Capt. Pauline Kirby (later promoted to major) and Capt. Mary Parker, both of whom we will meet again.

Wearing the civilian wool skirts and coats in which they had embarked, and ordered not to bring a change of clothing, the nurses learned that promised uniforms had not been delivered on board. The PX on every ship had also failed to stock sanitary napkins. Mary Connell debarked at Panama and bought her nurses linen romper suits with skirts and enough Kotex for the whole "fleet."

They landed in Brisbane, and the various units were sent in all directions. The 5th Station Hospital group stayed together, moving from Melbourne to Perth to Canberra within six months. In the meantime many other nurses came to the continent, among them a few who had escaped from the Philippines.

At the end of April 1942, and just before the fall of Corregidor,

MacArthur managed to send two Navy PBY patrol bombers from Australia to The Rock to bring out civilian dependents, older officers, and a few staff experts. Gen. Jonathan Wainwright, commander of the U.S. forces, put seventy people aboard the two planes, including twenty Army nurses. An additional eleven Army nurses and one Navy nurse escaped several days later on the submarine USS *Spearfish*.

One plane carrying ten of the nurses was disabled when refueling on Mindanao, and the  passengers were later captured. When the ten nurses in the other plane reached Darwin, they discovered that they were the only women in the bomb-torn city; all civilians had long since fled. Two of the nurses, 2nd Lt. Willa Hook and 2nd Lt. Catherine Acorn, persuaded their superiors to let them remain in Australia "to be among the first to go back to Manila." The rest returned to the States.

Toward the end of May the eleven nurses who had escaped by submarine arrived in Fremantle and were brought by tanker to Perth. Mary Connell met them and took them to the nurses' quarters. She said, "They had men's shoes on, men's trousers cut off at the knee, and men's shirts. [They had been out seventeen] days ... and never saw daylight until they reached Perth."

They were examined, and those judged fit for duty had the choice of staying or going home. One of them, 2nd Lt. Hortense McKay, stayed on. She later told how she ended up in Sydney assigned to the office of the chief surgeon in the base headquarters there. She remained for three years filling a variety of administrative chores, locating  suitable quarters for new nurse arrivals, arranging for their recreation while they awaited assignments, and making sure they stayed in uniform.

Uniforms turned out to be one of her chief concerns. The esprit de corps of nurses in towns and cities depended on standard uniforms that fit. Many of the nurses had landed in winter wool when they found themselves needing clothes for the tropics — culottes, head gear, shoes, slacks, long-sleeved shirts. Not much was coming from the United States, but shortages could be met by Australian manufacturers under reverse lend lease.

A report on SWPA prepared years later by Nola Forrest and Eileen Brady, who worked with her in the theater, gave a broader picture of the influx of hospitals and nurses. In February 1942 an Army affiliate — the 4th General Hospital from Western Reserve University in Ohio — arrived and set up in Melbourne. It became the largest and best equipped hospital in Australia with two thousand beds. Several station hospitals followed, as well as a group of surgical and evacuation hospitals, all in place by April.

The 118th General Hospital, an affiliate from Johns Hopkins in Baltimore, Maryland, went to Sydney in June, and the nurses were billeted in the Oriental Hotel at King's Cross. Thirty-six hours after their arrival, the Japanese shelled Sydney, and these nurses were among the few Americans to hear Japanese gunfire in Australia.

By the end of the year the total of American hospitals reached twenty-three, and as the months went on even rural regions with small towns found "the grounds ... dotted with numerous wards under construction." For many nurses these early days were a restless waiting period, as described by one of them.

Second Lieutenant Erma Meyers from Cleveland, Ohio, was among a group of 343 Army nurses who left New York on March 1, 1942 in a large convoy. Disembarking at Melbourne on April 10th, she was assigned with fifty-six others to the 28th Surgical Hospital, which was not yet activated. For three weeks she and her friends went shopping in the city, tried out Australian dishes and drinks in the local bars and restaurants, and groped their way through darkened streets at night to the Palm Grove and the Embassy Club with their big swing bands. Here they found partners from all the Allied countries eager to dance with American women.

Ordered to move at month's end, Erma departed for Camp Darley, Victoria, with three bottles of Scotch in her musette bag. Her group was greeted at the railroad station by "the big chief nurse herself," Capt. Martha Jane Clement. This "heavy-set woman in her middle fifties, surveyed us severely, wished us bon voyage, told us to be brave in whatever dangers we would meet ... and, in general, handed out the old BS," Erma told her diary.

Their camp was in a flat valley surrounded by windswept mountains, and the nurses were billeted in drafty quarters. Erma wrote, "As night drew on, it got colder and colder and colder. Sleep was practically impossible ... We never got completely undressed. Food was a succession of mutton, mutton, and mutton." Each month found the cold increasing as with the approach of fall, "An almost unbearable damp chill that creeps through to your bones ... the rain blows through the vents and cracks in the walls.

"Days were spent in drilling, marching, classes in Army etiquette, and loafing. There was very little work to be done in the tiny hospital as most of our patients had been Aussie soldiers," now recovered. Brighter moments were spent at the Aussie Officers Club in the evenings, going on picnics, visiting the nearby town of Bacchus Marsh, and enjoying male attention.

After three months the entire unit was quarantined for meningitis in the 4th General Hospital in Melbourne, where the young women went wild with boredom. They were released in the winter of mid-August and sent via two rail systems to Brisbane where they were installed not far away at Camp Columbia, the largest camp in Queensland. Here the "night air [was] extremely damp and chill, penetrating through blankets, numbing our feet," although the sun at midday was "fierce."

For social life an hour's train ride took the nurses into Brisbane, which Erma described as "pure Aussie" compared with the English propriety of Melbourne. Here Lennon's Hotel was the central meeting place for all Americans. In the lounge Erma met doctors from her outfit for drinks and the latest exchange of rumors.

By October 1942 she found herself attached to the 42nd General Hospital in Brisbane. This affiliate of the University of Maryland functioned as both a general and a station hospital. With men going north and nurses remaining behind, many of the latter were placed there on temporary duty. A number of months passed before Erma was assigned to her permanent post on Goodenough Island near Milne Bay.

Hospitals were constantly shifting as new bases were established in New Guinea. In 1943, Port Moresby, originally Base A, passed its service peak and turned over the American sick and wounded to hospitals in Australia. Milne Bay became the new Base A with Capt. Eileen Brady as chief nurse. By the spring of 1944 five station hospitals and six general hospitals were clustered at this huge staging area, standing by for further orders. At one point seven hundred nurses were quartered there, anxious to get to work while they endured the incessant rain, mud, and mosquitoes.

Oro Bay became Base B, and Mary Connell was sent to advance headquarters there as the chief nurse of NUGSEC, New Guinea Base Section. She traveled frequently to inspect hospitals in the region. When stationed on the base, she slept in a tent with chicken wire stretched over the top to keep the coconuts from landing on her head. She was occupied with the well-being of the nurses and with their supplies — especially the limited availability of sanitary napkins. Lower shipping priorities for the Pacific produced many shortages. "We were stepchildren," she said. "Everything went to Europe."

For interbase service two Dutch liners were converted to hospital ships, which carried medical supplies and personnel from Australia to New Guinea, returning to Australia with patients. To prepare against ship abandonment nurses were trained to handle lifeboats, climb rope ladders, and participate in boat drills. In 1943 the *Tasman* made her maiden voyage from Brisbane to Milne Bay, transporting the 47th Station Hospital personnel and equipment. The ship had a Dutch captain and a Javanese crew. In the last three months of that year she carried twelve hundred medical passengers and evacuated 365 patients. In February 1944 nurses boarded the *Maetsuycker* in Sydney bound for Milne Bay and points north. This ship also had a Dutch captain and Javanese crew. Her primary duty was to evacuate patients from forward areas in New Guinea to hospitals in the rear.

By mid-1944, Milne Bay was no longer a major base. The three chief bases were Finschhafen, Hollandia, and Biak, immense supply centers with port facilities and staging areas. There the general hospitals absorbed the personnel of former station hospitals and were part of clusters of hospitals caring for the stream of casualties pouring in from combat zones.

Hortense McKay described the way people in Australia were constantly coming and going, many heading north. That fall she found herself receiving orders to move to New Guinea, and on her last night in Sydney she gave a party for six nurses in her one-room apartment. She was following the local practice of arranging a dinner in her home with a menu that bypassed the unappetizing restaurant fare of the austerity program. One of her guests was Col. Nola Forrest, like the hostess a native of Minnesota.

The director of SWPA nurses, after six weeks of commuting between medical centers in Australia, was also given travel authority to move north. She was to arrive in Hollandia no later than October 9th to "assist in reorganization of general hospitals." The next day Nola flew out. She did not return to Australia until many years after the war.

# CHAPTER 6

# VOYAGE TO LEYTE

A s soon as Colonel Forrest landed in Hollandia, she found herself making travel plans. "Perhaps some commanding officer would call and ask me if I could come up, they were having trouble. It might be sickness, it might be that one of the nurses had to be returned to the States. Or maybe a commanding officer didn't get along with his chief nurse and what could he do about that. I was in my own tent maybe a couple of nights a week."

Hollandia had been in Allied hands for six months, and two years of intense struggle preceded Nola's arrival. The first weeks of 1943 saw the end of the Papua campaign, but the cost for the Allied troops had been high: almost one-third killed or wounded, one-half incapacitated when illness was counted in. In the next eighteen months SWPA forces pushed their way further up the coast, usually with excruciating effort. Hospitals were installed behind them in the wake of battle.

In October 1944 this largest military base was described as "an anthill of activity, with tractors plowing out the jungle day and night." Three hospitals were closing down and their nursing staffs were moving into three general hospitals that had recently expanded. Two new station hospitals were under construction, and medical specialists were putting them together. "[P]rofessors of surgery operated concrete mixers and bulldozers, enlisted medics hammered and sawed, and mosquito control units spent their days at carpentry rather than fighting malaria," to quote the official Army history. Nurses, while waiting for assignment, were placed in any active treatment center.

The New Guinea campaign was fought in stages. In early 1943, once Buna was secured, the Allies moved to the next stage, to take Lae. In an engagement later known as the Battle of the Bismarck Sea, they sent available aircraft against Japanese troop landing at the harbor. In March the Allied pilots wiped out almost an entire Japanese division. This marked the turning point to defensive warfare for the enemy, but neither side had the reserves to force a decisive victory.

Soldiers lurched in the jungle wilds through tangled overgrowth in semi-darkness, fearing ambush and sudden death. "Men on both sides collapsed exhausted from the debilitating tropical heat and humidity; soldiers shook violently from malarial chills or from drenchings in tropical downpours. Others simply went mad," according to the Army history. The monotonous field ration, which consisted of bully beef and biscuits for the Australians and cold, unappetizing C rations for the Americans, led to malnutrition for the heavily laden soldiers and susceptibility to the host of tropical diseases that thrived in the jungle moisture.

Every subsequent gain for the Allies was hard-won. Lae was finally occupied in June, but when the Australians drove the Japanese to Finschhafen fifty miles to the east, their troops fought all summer long taking out enemy pockets. Finally able to occupy the Finschhaven area that September, they continued to repel counterattacks from entrenched enemy troops.

By this time, however, Allied troop strength had vastly increased, and the rate of advance improved. In January 1944 the Japanese were forced to withdraw to the mountains one hundred miles up the coastline at Saidor, leaving behind their code books half-hidden in a metal trunk in a stream. The discovery enabled Allied cryptanalysts in Brisbane to solve the enemy's main cipher system. MacArthur could take advantage of this intelligence windfall to make a calculated jump of four hundred miles behind enemy lines to Hollandia. This major Japanese air and supply base was lightly held, and after American bombers destroyed enemy aircraft on the ground, the infantry landed unopposed in April.

Meanwhile the Allies had moved on Aitape 140 miles southeast of Hollandia, where the fighting was intense and lasted for several months.

Nine out of ten Allied soldiers, unable to bathe, suffered skin diseases without relief. Their intestines became infected with worms, and psychiatric cases rose, especially among newer troops unused to jungle warfare.

While Hollandia had fallen easily and had an excellent harbor, the terrain was too soft to support the impact of planes as heavy as B-17s and B-24s. Needed airstrips could be provided by the island of Biak, with its coral reefs, 225 miles away to the west. In May the Americans landed their first wave on this island.

They took a heavy pounding of mortar and artillery fire from the enemy entrenched in a 200-foot-high cliff above the coast road and later met furious attacks from Japanese deep in caves to the east and west. Fighting continued until mid-July, by which time the casualties on the American side had reached nearly twenty-eight hundred.

As Biak was resisting capture, MacArthur ordered his forces to take enemy airstrips on the tiny island of Noemfoor, sixty miles to the south. By this action he could fly bombers and send troops to the westernmost end of New Guinea to capture Sansapor on the Vogelkop Peninsula by July 30th. To tighten his hold, he sent troops further west to seize the island of Morotai in Indonesia. This provided a site for airfields and radar stations for use in the coming assault on the Philippines.

The only remaining holdouts were Wewak and Aitape. Here intense fighting continued until August, making this was the most costly engagement since the capture of Buna with three thousand American casualties (versus ten thousand Japanese killed). Wewak held out until May 1945. Everywhere in New Guinea the effort had called for great sacrifice, marked by the number of Medals of Honor awarded, many posthumously, and other battle decorations, often won by members of medical units.

Once major conflict subsided on Biak, Army nurses came from Goodenough Island near Milne Bay with five hospitals to care for the casualties — three general hospitals and a station hospital plus an evacuation hospital that was placed on the nearby island of Owi. Eileen Brady was the base section chief of this entire group.

Later on, Colonel Forrest paid a visit to Biak and was struck by the ferocity of the battle that had taken place. "The Japanese went into caves," she said, "and then when our troops came, they came out of the caves and slaughtered them." The island was sixty miles south of the equator, and palm trees grew out from coral beds. When Nola was there, the sun almost never seemed to set.

She was visiting hospital centers at the end of the chain of evacuation. This system was designed to offer wounded men a series of treatments after they were first moved away from combat areas. In battalion aid stations near the front line they were treated for shock and their wounds were dressed, and if these were not serious, a man might return to battle. Otherwise he would move on to a collecting station where he might receive a blood transfusion and perhaps preliminary surgery. In a clearing station he could receive more complex treatment and a reliable prognosis. In a field hospital, a few miles to the rear, he would undergo more advanced surgery. If his case was serious, he would be moved to an evacuation hospital, then transported to a fixed hospital to recuperate or, if no longer fit for combat, sent home.

In the New Guinea jungle this system was short-circuited by the conditions of warfare. The military advance along the coast was, by necessity, amphibious — marching to meet the enemy through heavy growth on mountain slopes was not an option. Troops landed on the coastline, and medics and doctors treated casualties in aid stations and portable hospitals set up ashore. Medics transferred seriously wounded patients to LSTs (landing ship, tanks) and smaller craft. These became impromptu waterborne ambulances that moved the sick and wounded to established bases.

The 360th Station Hospital on Goodenough Island was a center on one such base. Here Erma Meyers worked from the end of 1943 until she became ill the following year. She described the scene in several letters home: "The camp itself is located in a really beautiful spot [with] fantastically colorful sunrises and sunsets ... facing me is a range of huge mountains ... here are beautiful mountain streams with cold, lovely water, but we can't drink it. So we're back to the old Lister [Lyster] bag again." She mentioned feeling "awfully small" wading through the kunai grass and spoke of the "extremely fatiguing tropical weather" that made it "impossible to move about quickly."

The wards were "in huge grass thatched huts, and very busy." She told how the nurses worked twelve to fourteen hours at a stretch when patient loads were heavy. Her day started at 6 a.m. in the dark when she donned her uniform of "khaki slacks, high canvas leggings, a cute little shirt called a 'safari' jacket ... reaching to your hips with big pockets, and my bile green 'Jeep' hat."

Of scrub typhus cases she noted, "The patients are so terribly sick, and there is so little we can do for them. It breaks my heart to watch them die." It was "still the rainy season — torrents every day. The whole damn island is a sea of mud ... I slide and slip in it all nite long ... as soon as darkness falls huge sheets of lightening start to flash." The dehydrated food, which Erma described as "the worst tasting stuff I've ever attempted to eat," added to the misery.

By April 1944, still busy, she had five wards to cover one night and described how "[A]n officer ... cutting himself a mosquito bar with his machete ... had cut off his entire hand. Then a poor GI was brought in with a broken back ... developed an acute appendix and had to be taken to surgery, his body cast cut off, then his belly cut open ... Add to that a few bad malarias, a poison case, a few burns, five fellows who walked on a land mine, some jungle rot, some goldbricks ... and you can see what a problem I had."

By this time, however, Erma was getting help from the healing power of penicillin, a newly developed antibiotic. This "miracle drug" first appeared in the SWPA region in November 1943 and within two years was widely available to all the theater medical units. More effectively than sulfa drugs, it eliminated diseases ranging from TB and pneumonia to gonorrhea, bringing recovery from multiple infections to thousands of men.

·+ ᘓᑯ·+᙭᙭·+ ·+

In her inspection rounds Nola Forrest set out from her headquarters in Hollandia with its huge hospital complex. For daily living " ... they gave us an area in the WAC [Women's Army Corps] compound. It was just myself and, I think, four in my office. We had three tents, one a tent office with all the records. Your showers were probably a block away, and the water was just ice cold. It was very hot in New Guinea, tropical, and to get up in the morning when it was a little bit coolish anyhow and go and get this ice cold . . .! Outside there was a big Lyster bag of [chemically treated] drinking water, which was warm, always.

You never had cold water to drink. That could have been reversed a little — to get your cold water to drink and your showers a little bit warm wouldn't have been so bad."

The WAC living area was enclosed by a high fence and patrolled twenty-four hours a day. Except for going back and forth to work, women were allowed out of the compound only with male escorts, usually in pairs, and the escorts wore sidearms. Travel was usually by jeep, and the order was to remain on traveled roads. A curfew required all the military women, including the nurses, to be in their compound by 10:00 p.m.

"We ate in the mess hall with all the other people in headquarters," Nola went on, "not with the WACs. We were the only women. We ate with our group and with mess kits. The food was very, very poor. Let's see ... it's something I want to blot out. They sometimes had stew, and sometimes they would serve it out of ... like a big garbage can. They would dip it out and put it in your bowl on your tray as you went by. Sometimes we had bread. We hardly ever had vegetables. We had C rations most of the time — powdered eggs. You see, they were trying to put all their supplies on those ships that were leaving."

Clothing was wet from perspiration. Faces turned yellow from Atabrine. But beauty parlors helped morale and were sorely needed. The red New Guinea clay could blow into hair as dust and stick to clothing as mud. "Frankly," one male officer was heard to remark, "women who had looked very well in Australia looked like hell in Hollandia."

There preparations for the invasion of Leyte were moving toward a climax. The harbor was full of ships being put in readiness to sail eighteen hundred miles away to the northwest. The whole area swarmed with military men, WAC office workers, native laborers, Red Cross women, soldiers, naval personnel, nurses, and supply technicians.

Engineers had built a road from the port two thousand feet up the slope of a mountain above the waters of Lake Sentani. At the end of the road they had constructed a white, prefab headquarters for MacArthur along with a number of other buildings. Most of the general's staff were quartered here while MacArthur himself was in Brisbane making final plans for his return to the Philippines.

On the morning of October 21st, Nola received a telephone call from Col. Paul Brickey, a medical officer attached to Gen. Walter Krueger's Sixth Army. He said, "We're getting two field hospitals with nurses on one of those ships going into Leyte. I'm not supposed to tell you this."

The nurses were moving under secret orders on a ship at the outermost edge of the harbor. It was one of more than seven hundred vessels, including battleships, LSTs, cruisers, destroyers, three kinds of aircraft carriers, minesweepers, transport ships, and a host of service craft, which together made up the Philippine Task Force.

This huge armada had been rapidly assembled upon a decision by the highest command to move the Leyte invasion to October instead of November, as originally planned. In mid-September, sorties from Admiral William F. ("Bull") Halsey's Third Fleet aircraft carriers had destroyed an unexpectedly large number of enemy planes and ships in the Central Philippines, and reconnaissance flights over Leyte had shown that few Japanese troops appeared to be garrisoned on the island. This information relayed to the joint chiefs of staff in Washington brought about a rapid change in plans. They decided to join most of the forces assigned to MacArthur and Nimitz in a huge amphibious enterprise.

An expert planning staff started to work around the clock to produce a detailed operational schedule for the departure of ships from scattered locations in the Pacific, each one to arrive with precise timing in Leyte Gulf. The "time table" was more than one inch thick when completed, and according to one source, "It took four pages just to list who was to get copies."

Brickey's telephone call was a signal to Nola. As she was leaving for her overseas assignment Surgeon General Norman T. Kirk had instructed her to get the nurses in soon after an invasion to "give good help early" and save lives. Now she went to General Denit and said, "I think I should go in, too." He replied, "I should say not. You can't go."

Hospitals under his authority within USASOS could be ordered out by combat commands. The two field hospitals with nurses had been called in by the Sixth Army surgeon, Col. William Hagins, to support the invasion, and it is not clear whether General Denit even knew of the order. He was once quoted as saying, "I sometimes got a chance to review and comment, but no amount of pleading could change things if the CG, task forces, ruled otherwise."

Although not attached to a hospital, Nola could make a strong case for her presence in this initial use of nurses in a combat area, pointing out that her presence could justify the decision. "I reminded Denit and his assistant of the wishes of General Kirk and finally I got them to say all right." The orders were cut on the spot. Nola later learned that Colonel Hagins had requested her.

Within two days she set out in a launch with Eileen Brady, whom she had asked to come down from Biak and help in the office in her absence. For breakfast they were given one Vienna sausage and a cup of watered down coffee with no bread.

The ship was the USS *John Alden*, and it was anchored twelve miles offshore. The two women were carried out in a choppy sea. Well, Nola thought, we can get there, but how are we going to get on? As they pulled away, she remembered seeing stacks of mail piled up on the shore, soaking in the rain, and wondered if the letters would ever be delivered.

When they reached the *John Alden*, "My heart sank," said Nola. "There was a rope ladder down the side of the ship a great distance, and it was rough. We were going this way and that way, and it was still raining. I've always hated water anyhow. I thought, oh, my laws!

"We were trying to find a calm moment when I could leap over the water and grab hold of the ladder. They managed to get me to grab the rope, which was slippery, and the soldiers were up there watching, you know, and it looked like it was a mile up to climb. They'd say, 'Come on, colonel, come on. Now rest. Don't worry, you can make it. You just have to keep going.' When I got far enough for them to get hold of my hand, a couple of them grabbed me and pulled me over.

"And talk about uniforms — the only thing we could wear out there were these heavy, twill khaki pants and blouses, long sleeves and leggings, and high-top shoes! They sent a rope down for my Valpack, and they got that up."

Eileen Brady went up the ladder next amid considerable ribbing from the soldiers, who told her she'd never make it. Once she saw Nola safely aboard, she was taken back to Hollandia.

The *John Alden* was a Liberty ship. Named for notable (deceased) Americans, the Liberty ships were based on a tramp steamer design, and during the war the Navy converted a number of them to auxiliary configuration. The vessels usually operated with an armed guard of ten to twenty sailors in addition to the ship's crew and served as hospital ships, cargo ships, repair ships, prisoner-of-war transports, mule transports, and troop ships, among other uses. They had a relatively slow rate of speed.

The *John Alden* had been reshuffled with other groups in the Pacific to enlarge the Seventh Fleet commanded by Adm. Thomas C. Kinkaid, who served under MacArthur. No harbor was large enough to accommodate all of the ships. They were staged at various locations, then brought together according to schedule.

This voyage had started out in Finschhafen, picking up some nurses and enlisted men, and then stopping for a layover in Aitape. The next leg of the voyage took the ship to Hollandia, where it rested at anchor for five days. Departure from Hollandia was on October 23rd.

The *John Alden* was on the outer edge of a large convoy with no other ships on one side. During six days en route Nola kept her mind focused "playing bridge a lot down in the dining room — just the table where we ate and two benches with no backs on them." The ship was blacked out at night, which made for stifling heat as the players continued their game.

Nola's companions were two doctors and Capt. Claire Whalen, chief nurse of the 1st Field Hospital, who would later marry her bridge partner. (The chief nurse of the 2d Field Hospital was Capt. Catherine Acorn, getting her wish to return to the Philippines.) As high-ranking officers the bridge players had a table to themselves, and they continued their contest whenever they weren't eating or sleeping or being interrupted by the general alarm, which sounded day and night.

While they played, Tokyo Rose came on the radio. "I have some news for you," she announced. "Twenty-seven nurses are going to the Philippines, and, you poor girls, you'll never see your homes again." Then she started in on the men.

The ship's engineer watched their game. He liked Nola and every evening would bring her a Coke with ice in it. "Here were my friends with their tongues hanging out," said she, "so I shared it with them." The scene unfolded as though in a dream. The engineer told them how his career had included stints as a bodyguard to Lance Reventlow, son of Barbara Hutton, and another as a dealer in stolen goods. He asked Nola if she wanted any furs; he could get some through a fence he knew in New York

City. He also offered her the use of his cabin for a shower. Nola tactfully declined his invitation — she would use a shower assigned to the women.

She was quartered in a "little hole" they had fixed for her on the deck over the ship's rec room, and she had to climb up three or four steps to reach it. She could remember the soldiers singing noisily right beneath her bed and that "[w]hen the general alarm sounded, I had to run down those steps and go inside the ship and lie on the floor. One night I got halfway down — of course, you never took your clothes off — and discovered I didn't have my glasses, which I kept under my pillow. I can't see a thing without my glasses. Up I go, and here's the alarm going ooga, ooga, ooga, and you can hear the bombs dropping, and I got my glasses, and I got down inside again. I always tried to lie near a little married nurse who was terrified."

Nola claimed to have felt no fear during those alarms — she was in a state of exhilaration, "having fun." Her nature seemed to include an underlying belief that things would turn out all right. The intensity of the moment outweighed any thoughts of pain and death.

As the *John Alden* steamed toward its destination, the battle of Leyte Gulf was raging in waters close to the island. This gigantic encounter took place over four days, October 23rd to 26th. When it thundered to a close, it ranked as the greatest naval engagement in history.

On October 20th the first U.S. invasion convoys had begun to unload at Leyte. That same day General MacArthur splashed shore and announced his return to the Philippines. Two days later he declared Tacloban the temporary capital of the country and swore in Sergio Osmena, former president of the islands, as president once again.

Meanwhile the Japanese naval command, aware that the Americans were assembling a large invasion force, decided to launch the "decisive battle" of the war in a last stand to thwart the U.S. effort. Not sure of the landing site, they were able to crystallize their plans as soon as MacArthur stepped ashore at Tacloban and made his announcement.

Their strategy was to advance three large naval formations from different starting points to converge in a pincer movement in Leyte Gulf, causing heavy damage to U.S. naval forces and undermining the American attack on the island. One group would sail eastward from Borneo and another would sail southeast from Okinawa, joining forces

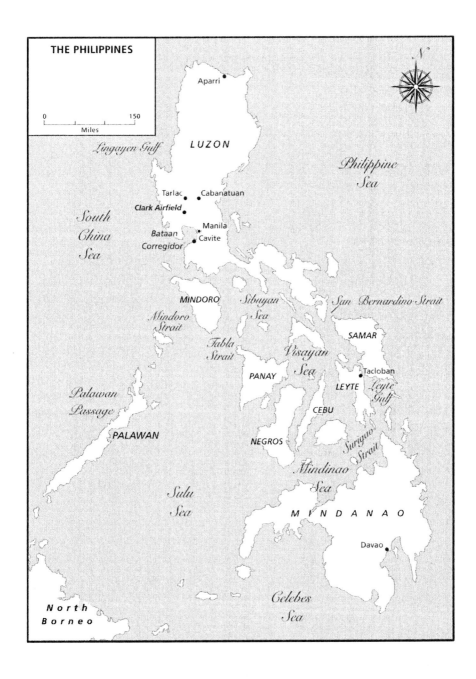

THE PHILIPPINES

0 ——————— 150
Miles

Aparri

LUZON

Lingayen Gulf

South
China
Sea

Tarlac   Cabanatuan
Clark Airfield
Manila
Bataan   Cavite
Corregidor

Philippine
Sea

MINDORO   Sibuyan
Sea

San Bernardino Strait

Mindoro
Strait

Tabla
Strait

Visayan
Sea

SAMAR

PANAY

Tacloban

LEYTE   Leyte
Gulf

Palawan
Passage

CEBU

PALAWAN

NEGROS

Surigao
Strait

Mindinao
Sea

Sulu
Sea

MINDANAO

Davao

North
Borneo

Celebes
Sea

to proceed one after the other through Surigao Strait, then turning north toward the gulf. The third and largest formation under Vice Admiral Takeo Kurita would sail from Sumatra, heading northeast toward and through San Bernardino Strait around the island of Samar. Turning south, Kurita would join the other Japanese warships in an ultimate and punishing battle with the U.S. Seventh Fleet.

When the Americans began to unload in Leyte Gulf, they were unaware of the location of the Japanese navy. By October 22nd, Admiral Kurita was moving his flotilla northeast past Palawan, the southwesternmost island of the Philippine archipelago. Here U.S. submariners positioned in those waters were taken by surprise. With great presence of mind, they discharged one torpedo after another in the direction of the enemy ships, inflicting considerable damage.

Undeterred by these attacks, Kurita pressed on into the Sibuyan Sea on his way to the strait, and here he met powerful air resistance from American pilots who had been alerted to his route. He sustained serious losses, including the sinking of his flagship, but he still continued on his course.

At the southern end of Leyte the commanders of the U.S. Seventh Fleet had lined up destroyers, cruisers and battleships to block the Japanese advance through Surigao Strait. As assaults from the American forces were sinking and turning back these warships, Kurita continued to push his badly damaged fleet through San Bernardino Strait in the north. Here he found his passage unexpectedly peaceful.

On October 25th, as he turned his force south toward Leyte Gulf, he was met by a group of destroyers and small U.S. escort carriers that launched an attack on these far larger ships in a heroic delaying action. Confused by a false impression of the size of the defenders, Kurita retreated and headed back through the strait. Admiral Halsey's Third Fleet might have joined the action but was diverted by a fourth Japanese naval group moving toward the gulf from the Philippine Sea.

Kamikaze pilots launched the first suicide attacks in the midst of the conflict. When the sacrificial pilots hit their floating targets, the resulting explosions caused terrible firestorms and agonizing deaths for American sailors. Despite their unnerving power  these attacks did not turn the tide of battle. The bulk of the enemy fleet was sunk, including three battleships, four carriers, nine cruisers, twelve destroyers, and hundreds of aircraft. The loss of manpower ran into the thousands. The Americans sustained the destruction of seven combat ships, including three carriers, and the loss of hundreds of men.

On October 29th the *John Alden* was in the midst of a convoy of support ships that were reaching Tacloban harbor on San Pedro Bay just off the gulf. The Japanese mounted air attacks in the midst of a heavy storm, the worst typhoon in recent memory. The noise was deafening. The wind was blowing at ninety miles per hour, and the captain was forced to put out two anchor ropes, one on each end of the ship, and keep the engines running at full speed to hold the vessel upright.

"We spent two days and two nights in the harbor with the Japanese after us all the time," Nola stated in an article in *The American Journal of Nursing*. "The first night was terrifying as a ship on one side of us exploded and one on the other side sank, and we expected to be rammed by other ships every moment. Our ship was silhouetted between a flaming gas dump and the full moon, and we were a perfect target."

After two sleepless nights, Nola and the nurses were able to disembark at daybreak during a lull. A truck was waiting for them, and the first words they heard were, "Now, the minute the truck stops, jump out and hide in a rice paddy." They were being driven ten miles south of Tacloban to Palo, and they had to jump out only once under threat of attack.

Three hours after their landing they were at work. "The nurses proceeded to the improvised hospital wards and commenced bathing and dressing the patients," Nola later reported. "When we arrived, the patients were haggard and harassed. The Medical Department men had done a wonderful job but could not give the patients individual care. The next day it was a transformed hospital. The patients were smiling, smoking, and had lost that worried look. Many said it was the first bath they had had in twelve days."

In Palo the two field hospitals, unable to unload their equipment, joined forces with the 36th Evacuation Hospital, which had set up its operations in the San Salvador Cathedral. This hospital was part of a 20-unit medical group sent in to serve the X Corps of the Sixth Army. The casualties were fresh from the fighting that began on October 20th, when the first troops landed.

The infantry had to push through a wretched environment to take airfields, hills, and towns. Operations "were carried out in torrential rains which turned dirt roads into sloughs, open fields into swamps and rice paddies into mud ponds," wrote historian Samuel Eliot Morison. The soldiers met counterattacks from the air and fanatically resisting Japanese troops on land.

One hundred and fifty of the most seriously wounded men were placed in the main body of the Palo cathedral, and the rest of the patients were in tents outside. The surgeons used the baptismal font to scrub. The 200-year-old cathedral, said to be the oldest Christian church in the Philippines, was still being used for worship. Every morning at 7:30 a priest conducted mass, and three masses were held on Sundays. Nola wrote to Colonel Blanchfield that it was "a colorful sight to see the Filipinos in their white starched suits and dernas with the black and white veils taking communion while the nurses were serving the patients breakfast."

"For the first two days, we didn't have control of the air," Nola explained. "Still we had to go in line to get our food. They had soup in a great big drum, and they'd scoop it out and give it to you. There would be a Japanese chap, reconnaissance, one they used to call Charlie the Washing Machine Man, who would be chug, chug, chugging over us, looking over the place. We'd kind of laugh at him."

Charlie went away, but "one evening," wrote Nola, "a lone Zero dropped a bomb and strafed people a half block from the hospital, and about twenty were mutilated. This same plane dived and strafed the front door of the hospital. However, the bullets, instead of going in the door, struck the outside and ricocheted, causing small nicks in the shoulders and arms of some patients."

"As I looked up," Nola recalled, "I could see the fellow's face. He dived down to our nurses' [working] tent outside the hospital. We all dropped to the floor inside. I guess I was on the bottom. Finally one of the nurses said, 'Are you all right, colonel? I haven't felt you breathing for a long time.' "

The staff was certain the enemy would come over in full force when darkness fell. That night the nurses, who were billeted nearby in a nipa shack raised up on stilts with a carabao grunting beneath it, moved into the cathedral. They tried to sleep on the marble floor of the altar, and they were joined by a number of Filipino civilians seeking shelter.

Capt. Nola Forrest with Lt. Edna Traeger, Army War Show, summer 1942 (*Des Moines Register*— Nola Forrest papers)

Maj. Nola Forrest, promoted March 25, 1943 (Nola Forrest papers)

Lt. Margaret Decker, 127th Station Hospital, Desert Training Center, Needles, CA, awarded the Soldier's Medal, June 19, 1943 (Nola standing extreme right) (ANC/U.S. Army)

Lt. Col. Nola Forrest, promoted February 29, 1944 (National Archives)

I.D. card, issued July 7, 1944 (Nola Forrest papers)

Travel orders, Brisbane to Melbourne and Sydney, September 9, 1944 (Nola Forrest papers)

2nd Lt. Erma Myers, 1943 (courtesy Robert Aarons)

U.S. Army nurses on hospital ship in New Guinea, 1942 (National Archives)

Nola Forrest and Pauline Tobey with unidentified nurse, Hollandia New Guinea, 1944 (U.S. Signal Corps)

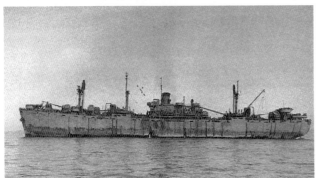

Liberty ship, SS *Carlos Carillo* (U.S. Navy)

Interior of San Salvador Cathedral, Palo, Leyte, site of the 36th Evacuation Hospital, November, 1944 (National Archives)

Nola Forrest alighting from
bomber, Lae, New Guinea,
November 16, 1944
(U.S.Signal Corps)

Nola Forrest and
Eileen Brady,
Hollandia, New
Guinea, 1944
(U.S. Signal
Corps)

Guest tents at the
126th General
Hospital near Palo,
Leyte (National
Archives)

Nola's head was under the bishop's chair, and she still remembered the dust in her nostrils. By her account, "No one got any sleep with the noise of our 90mm guns and the ack-ack. The Japs came over every five or ten minutes regularly all night. I counted about forty raids altogether."

The hospital cared for injured Filipinos and wounded Japanese soldiers along with the Americans. Nola was surprised to find movie actor Lew Ayres among the corpsmen. As a conscientious objector he was assigned as a chaplain's assistant, and he was one of the few hospital workers who were kind to the helpless Japanese. He consulted with Nola and devised a way to get the prisoners off the wet and muddy ground by hoisting their litters between adjacent trees.

The SWPA director felt the decision to bring nurses into a combat zone had been vindicated. By sending them into a forward area before it was safe, the Sixth Army's chief surgeon had departed from official policy despite the objections of General Krueger. Nola wrote to Colonel Blanchfield, "... the girls in this invasion certainly proved the value of post-operative nursing care ... I was so proud of the way the nurses operated through all the noise and enemy action ... [They] are doing a wonderful job. We hope to get more hospitals in soon." All of the nurses were awarded the Bronze Star for their performance during those critical days and nights.

After five intense days on Leyte, Nola was looking for a ride back to Hollandia. The field nurses had their work well in hand, and she needed to get back to New Guinea where she had only begun her inspection trips. As she recalled, "I knew the bomber head, General 'Jimmy' Crabbe, real well. I called him and I asked if he had anything. He said, 'I'm going back this afternoon. If you can get down to Tacloban, I'll send a jeep for you.' "

This arrangement was informal and Nola's trip to town was short, but military regulations require an order for every move. Among her papers we find a typewritten sentence on official stationery: "Permission is hereby granted for LT. COL. NOLA FORREST, ANC, to travel between Palo and Tacloban on Friday, 4th November 1944," signed by the military commander, 36th Evacuation Hospital.

CHAPTER 7

# NINE WEEKS
# IN NEW GUINEA

The flight back to New Guinea might have been the end. As the bomber was readying for takeoff between air attacks, Nola climbed aboard in a daze of exhaustion. She shifted into the upper part of the plane, designed to hold the pilot and co-pilot and one or two others. "General Crabbe had me sit up there with the airmen," she recalled. "He went down with the people in the bomb bay, some officers and war correspondents.

"That was the time we missed our mark. There is an island called Helen Island that they used as a navigation signal. After a while the pilots kept looking and talking, and I thought, my gosh, what's going on here, they looked so upset. So finally one of them went down and got General Crabbe, and he came up — they made him big pilot, see? It was real cold in that plane that night, and they put a coat around me. He saw I was kind of worried, and he patted me.

"Well, we finally landed down in Noemfoor, which was about two or three hundred miles from Hollandia. When I saw us going down, it was so brightly lighted and everything — I had heard about our planes going down in Halmahera in the Jap territory — I thought, wouldn't that be something!

"Once the plane touched ground, General Crabbe said, 'You're staying here tonight,' because I hadn't slept — I was a wreck. But we had a hospital in Noemfoor. I had been there before. So he called and had a car come down from the hospital and take me up to sleep. Then he sent a bomber back the next day. I got back to work on a Sunday morning."

By Nola's account her energy soon rebounded. She stated in her letter to Colonel Blanchfield that despite having had only eight hours of sleep in seven days, she had never felt better in her life, which must have been bravado. Whatever the reality, she was ready to embark on extended inspections.

The day she returned, orders were cut for her and Pauline Kirby to travel to areas both under USASOS control and "in the forward areas as necessary." This implied that they could call on hospitals in Leyte as well as New Guinea and could go aboard hospital ships.

Nola traveled from one end of New Guinea to the other. On some of her trips Major Kirby joined her, but she frequently traveled alone. She spoke of her assistant as "wonderful ... I could leave [her] behind in the office, and I knew everything would be taken care of the way I would like to have it. That's the best kind of assistant to have, one that doesn't change everything the minute you get out of the office."

Colonel Forrest was at the pinnacle of a hierarchy of chief nurses of bases and base sections, who visited the hospital groups within their areas every month. She conferred with them, as well as the doctors, interpreting theater policies. One time-consuming duty was the redistribution of nursing staff as patient loads kept changing. If problems could not be resolved locally, they were referred to higher levels.

In two months Nola flew to more than thirty hospitals up and down the length of the island, and on her flights the elevation of the aircraft provided relief from the tropical heat. "Of course, the only way you could travel was by plane," she explained, "and I was usually the only woman on the plane. It might be a cargo plane, or it might be a bomber. It might be anything that was going at the time I wanted to go up to see a hospital."

Male officers often carried cribbage boards in their pockets, and cribbage games en route provided a distraction from boredom or the discomfort of the bucket seats. Now and then the planes would descend suddenly from shifts in the wind or engine trouble, and Nola could remember a fatalistic feeling when this happened.

Her story kept growing as I called on her from year to year. On one occasion she had just passed her 96th birthday, and her room held vases full of fading flowers and a basket piled high with birthday cards. She was asleep in her chair, then woke up cheerfully, adjusted her wig, and welcomed me. Although her voice was barely audible, she answered my questions with careful attention.

I asked her about New Guinea, and as she recalled the scenery, she spoke of "beautiful rivers and beautiful mountains and then long stretches of just flat land. Of course, it was a country that we had never come in contact with before or even visualized or thought about. They had no roads. They had no type of civilized living at all."

She remembered the sites of some of her visits. "We got nurses into Biak and Noemfoor and into Sansapor, which is way up at the real top of New Guinea. Then we had Morotai, an island which is beyond the very end, only about five minutes' flying time from Halmahera, where the Japs were. And at night — first time I was up there inspecting a hospital — we were in this tent, all the tents had foxholes by them, and the minute a Jap plane started — we knew when the Japs left Halmahera to bomb over there — there would be three shots on a rifle or a gun, and that meant 'foxholes,' see? On the nights you'd hear that, out you'd go, and they would come over and bomb a little bit. Then, when one shot came, that meant 'all clear,' and you could go back to bed."

On this trip Nola brought Pauline Kirby along. In the foxhole they sat back to back talking to each other while the enemy rained missile after missile in their direction. Kirby wasn't fazed at all. "I wish they'd stop so I could go to bed,"she grumbled.

By November hospitals on New Guinea began to fill with casualties from the fighting on Leyte. Few beds on Leyte were functional, and the Army was forced to rely on LSTs and hospitals on troop ships for immediate treatment of the sick and wounded before transferring patients to hospital ships for evacuation. Lightly wounded men who would normally have been treated in Leyte hospitals, and perhaps returned to combat, found themselves sent to hospitals in New Guinea along with the heavily wounded.

Hospital ships were governed by regulations of the Geneva Convention of 1929 (not ratified by the Japanese). They were painted white with a broad green stripe along the hull and red crosses on the funnel, were brilliantly lighted at night, and were registered with the enemy. By late 1944 the theater boasted seven hospital ships, and every attack transport ship also had a small hospital with a medical staff aboard.

On October 25th the first patients arrived at the 54th General Hospital in Hollandia, and a technician described the day:

> The long string of ambulances that began steaming in late in the afternoon, the wounded patients lying there so silently, the hustle and bustle and noise and confusion. Plenty of us felt a strange sensation seeing the wounded with bitterness in their eyes, yet with ... relief written on their faces for having gotten out of it alive ... As the wee hours of the morning crept in ... all our first battle casualties were bedded down, and in the new light of morning, surgery started right in operating on a full schedule ... Although the hospital kept operating new wards ... sprawling out in all directions, there appeared on the surface a certain calmness ... Under that surface [one might see] the fight to save a man's life, a man's mind, a man's limb.

Growing to 3,500 beds, the 54th General Hospital became the Army's largest overseas medical facility. The nurses working there were drawn from twenty-two other hospitals to serve on temporary duty, and they "...soon became confident, self-reliant and dependable—a rapid transition from rookie to veteran," according to a medical officer's report.

The hospital ships began their round-trip schedules soon after the invasion. They were manned by Navy crews and staffed by Army medical teams. The first to enter the invasion area was the USS *Mercy*, with thirty-eight Army nurses, a dietitian, and two Red Cross women. She sailed from San Pedro Bay on October 26th with 410 patients, many suffering severe burns, took some to another ship and then went to Manus Island. She was back in Leyte Gulf in less than three weeks.

Three days later the USS *Comfort* picked up both Army and Navy patients from LSTs and took them to Hollandia. On November 7th the USS *Hope* arrived in the gulf, then returned again that month, taking patients to Hollandia both times. On her third trip she carried long-awaited nurses from New Guinea to Leyte where they disembarked on December 4th.

By Christmas Eve fresh food was delivered to the 54th General along with packages from home. The nurses and technicians were expecting to be off duty on time, and the officers had planned a party. Then news came in that another hospital ship had docked. The patients were the first group of abdominal, chest, and head cases returned from treatment centers on Leyte. Linens and blankets had to be found, new beds prepared, and blood plasma and fluids administered.

Nurses settled the most acutely ill in beds and surgeons examined them. The walking wounded soon felt better with hot food and Christmas cheer. As the evening wore on, the nurses scrambled to change dressings, schedule men for operations, administer penicillin and sufadiazine every four hours, get oxygen tents, feed the patients, make up beds, do charting, clean up the mud, and run errands, performing duties usually given to interns "in a manner which is the highest tribute to their training, ability ... and willingness to work," according to the report.

"Midnight comes, the surgery performed, transfusions given, drugs and dressing started, seriously ill reported as doing well, special nurses instructed. Then to the mess hail and choke down a few tired bites of food ... tomorrow is Christmas and those packages to be opened and the turkey dinner to be enjoyed." That morning another ship arrived with a load of the sick and wounded.

Nola was visiting hospitals like this one with staffs that were under heavy pressure. She was concerned with every aspect of the nurses' lives — illness, exhaustion, uniforms, recreation, living conditions, promotions, and relationships on different working levels. Acting as a troubleshooter, she consulted with the doctors who ran the hospitals and the chief nurses of hospitals and base sections.

Nola later wrote of the environment, "One could not find a more miserable, God-forsaken, unhealthy, and trying area in the world. The climate was hot, humid, and rainy. Certain areas registered the highest rainfall in the world ... The temperature in the hot and sticky climate ranged from 120 degrees during the day to 90 degrees at night after the sun had set."

The health of the nurses could be affected by the oppressive climate, the lack of privacy, skin abrasions from the damp protective cloth-ing, or just the distressing and repetitive nature of their work. For many women their menstrual periods became irregular or more intense, and for the flight nurses, more frequent. The unvaried and tasteless diet con-tributed to loss of weight and energy.

One nurse recalled a New Guinea barracks: "Thirty beds lined up in a row ... mosquito nets rolled nearby ... rain dripping from the eaves, limp raincoats hanging from mosquito bars ... clods of mud ... heavy, soggy shoes ... the smell of mildew ... irons cooling on the floor ... per-colators, gasoline stoves, electric grills ... onion sandwiches at midnight ... warm beer ... rumors, rumors, rumors .. yellow skins in the shower, the community latrine."

Health and morale were linked to the nature of the work, or the lack of it, and time spent in the theater. Living conditions with no access to privacy offered little chance for relaxation. The nurses felt chronic discomfort from the weight and rough texture of the uniforms. As time went on, increasing numbers of them were evacuated, more than half of these for pregnancy, neuropsychiatric conditions, and skin diseases, in that order.

In May 1944, Erma Meyers was one whose health was suffering. She underwent surgery for an ovarian cyst and an appendectomy. Two months later she was sent to Australia to recover from a virulent case of malaria and there met up with Ralph Aarons, a first lieutenant in the Chemical Warfare Service, whom she had known several years before. Within three weeks they found themselves in love and "after much red tape cutting" received permission to marry.

A memorandum from the captain of the Chemical Warfare School to the commanding general of the base went through channels. It read: "The undersigned has interviewed and explained to both parties desir-ing to marry, the difficulties and the many problems that arise from marriage in time of war ... He has investigated both parties and is of the opinion that the marriage has a reasonable chance of success and that regardless of the station of the officer, the dependents will not become public charges." Dated July 29, 1944, the piece of paper was formally approved by the next command.

An Australian military rabbi conducted an orthodox Jewish wed-ding service at the local temple in Brisbane, and friends of the bride and groom put on a lively post-nuptial reception with a 10-gallon keg of beer, ample baked goods, and strenuous dancing. Erma's leave was up that night, but in a devil-may-care mood she went AWOL (away without leave) to the beach with her husband.

The next day two MPs (military police) ordered her to report back to the base office where she was relieved to find that her commanding officer was extending her leave for five days. The honeymooners returned to the beach. Then Erma flew back to her post, and Ralph was ordered from temporary duty in the city to the Australian outback. Erma contrived to see Ralph once again on an unauthorized trip to Oro Bay, but by the end of the year she was in a hospital in the big Finschhafen base awaiting shipment to the States for exhaustion.

By the time Erma's overseas duty was ending, Nola Forrest had already put in almost three demanding months and would soon be undertaking a crucial mission. In her travels she relished a variety of human encounters, including many with the soldiers. "There are no patients in the world like the GI's," Nola once commented. "They're perfectly wonderful, and they adapt to everything. They're very willing to cooperate in every way with the nurses and with the corpsmen and with the doctors.

"It was very upsetting sometimes visiting those hospitals and seeing some of those heavily wounded men, still cheerful and asking us how long we'd been here. 'I'm going home next month,' they'd say, always thinking they would be going home … You never knew what would happen to them."

Nola also observed the local people. She remarked of the inhabitants, "I think they lived mostly by fishing, and they grew some sort of vegetable that they ate. The women seemed to do most of the work, and they were busy. The men wore nothing but G-strings, and the children wore nothing.

"By the time we got there, they were getting sort of used to people coming in, and they called everybody 'Joe.' It didn't matter where you went, it was 'Hello, Joe.' Or else, they'd put out their hands, they wanted something. We went and visited in several of the villages. That was up near Noemfoor and Sansapor where the Dutch had part of New Guinea."

The Dutch colonists welcomed the Allies as they liberated western New Guinea in the first seven months of 1944. Nola remembered an improvised meal. "One day the Dutch administrator up there asked us to dinner at his tent, and they had a little native boy with a string around his toe and a fan up above. He kept the fan going that way. The food was, well, it was poor. They always had a fried egg on top of everything, whether it was a piece of meat or ... and pass around a can of peaches in the can, and that was dessert."

On a trip to the lower end of the island near Milne Bay Nola visited the 268th Station Hospital. This 150-bed unit was served entirely by a black medical staff. The fifteen Army nurses were supervised by a chief nurse, Birdie Brown, whom Nola described as a "nice, jolly person." Whenever she opened the door of a ward, she would call out to the patients, "Attention! We have a very important visitor today!"

That night the colonel was invited to dinner with the staff. They were going to have a dance, and they asked Nola whether she was not too tired to attend and would perhaps like to rest. Not to put a damper on their party, she said would like to go to bed, she was getting up early.

In 1945 the Milne Bay hospital moved on to Manila. It was one of several Army hospitals in which African American nurses served overseas. One was near Monrovia, Liberia, where the 25th Station Hospital had an integrated unit of white physicians and black nurses. Another was a partially integrated hospital in England serving POWs, and still another was the 335th Station Hospital in Burma, staffed entirely by black medical personnel. By the end of the war 512 Negro nurses, as they were then called, were serving with the Army Nurse Corps.

Colonel Forrest recalled dinners at Finschhafen with some Dutch missionaries who had been caught there by the war and at Lae, fifty miles away, where the commanding officer presented Irving Berlin as a dinner companion. He was, according to Nola, "a charming man with a little old reedy voice," and he was flying from post to post entertaining the troops with his *This Is the Army* show.

After dinner they were invited to a sing-sing, put on by natives of a nearby village attired in scanty costumes of shells and feathers, chanting, dancing, and playing instruments to celebrate a special event. In the jeep on the way to the performance the composer asked Nola what she disliked most about the Army, and she replied, "The pants!" This remark inspired him to write a song which was later featured at a concert in Manila.

Nola's sociability gave her a lift from the weight of her duties, and she warmly remembered a special dinner hosted by the Navy. One Captain Kelly, commander of a naval hospital a few miles north of Hollandia, "came down to see me, and he said, 'We're going to have some nurses in. I want you to come up and see what you think about their quarters. Could I come down and get you for dinner ... on such-and such a night?' And I said yes.

"So we went up there," Nola recounted, "and the Seabees [naval construction battalions] had built a house for them, a nice house. The Seabees, of course, did everything. They did a lot for us, too. They were wonderful. Then we went to the dining room, and they sat us down at a table with tablecloths, and we were served their food, and it was a delicious steak we had. Of course, they got that often from the Navy ships out in the harbor. And ice cream ... well, I hadn't seen ice cream for ... and ice!

"We had a drink before dinner, and I said, 'You mean to say you have ice?' 'Oh, yes,' he said. 'Oh,' I said, 'what we wouldn't give for ice!' And he said, 'Just send your boy up here.' It was probably a mile or two miles up, so I sent a corpsman up there from the office every afternoon. I don't think he meant it for every day, but we took advantage that way. We got ice every day, and then we had ice cream. You see, everybody was allowed a six-pack of beer and some rum — Australian rum is terrible — every week or so. But if you could just have ice, even for water!"

<hr/>

While Nola Forrest was spending the last two months of 1944 visiting SWPA hospitals, the troops on the island of Leyte were waging a desperate campaign against the Japanese, who had brought in reinforcements. On October 20th four infantry divisions, comprising the X Corps and the XXIV Corps, landed on the Leyte beaches. They made up the Sixth Army under the overall command of Gen. Walter Krueger. Their first mission was to take the Tacloban and Dulag airfields and after that, to proceed inland.

The same day, MacArthur arrived and proceeded to set up his headquarters in a battered mansion belonging to an American named Walter Price, who was in Manila, interned early in the war. From this

house the general directed the Leyte campaign.

The prime objective of the X Corps was to capture the Leyte Valley to the west and south of Tacloban. Here MacArthur planned to establish air bases, supply dumps, and troop staging areas from which to strike at Japanese forces in any part of the Philippines, but the hostile terrain and heavy rainfall thwarted these plans. The Japanese bombed the soggy American airstrips continuously as well as the supply ships in San Pedro Bay. Within two weeks, Gen. Tomoyuki Yamashita moved units from other islands to double the number of the Japanese troops on Leyte, feeding them in at Ormoc on the west coast.

Elements of the XXIV Corps moved south along a narrow path, crossed the island, and reached the west coast, heading north toward Ormoc to meet elements of the X Corps heading south in a pincer movement to take that strategic harbor. In the center of Leyte other infantry groups were pushing hard to the edge of the mountains, and still others managed to achieve an amphibious thrust around the mountainous northeastern tip of the island. They landed near Carigara, a fishing village.

In every engagement conditions were miserable. The men had to push themselves and their equipment through hot and humid jungles. Rot lay below the greenery, and nauseating odors from the decaying vegetation often caused vomiting. On slippery, precipitous mountain paths, feet were slashed by the razor-sharp rocks, and the enemy could be around any corner.

During November the Allied troops launched a 3-week attack just west and south of Carigara to breech the Japanese defense lines on Breakneck Ridge. The contest was the fiercest in the Leyte campaign and draining for both sides. Thousands of Japanese were killed, and many Americans either killed or wounded as they fought during a typhoon followed by high winds and driving rain that produced mud slides, fallen trees, and serious problems in supply.

As in New Guinea, disease was the major foe: four times as many casualties as battle wounds for Allied soldiers were caused by malaria, scrub typhus (carried by rodents), dengue fever, and dysentery. Many wounds were infected from the bacterial soil. Swollen rivers overflowed, and some of the wounded drowned in pools of water before they could be rescued.

In mid-December a final effort to take the port of Ormoc and surrounding territory resulted in victory for Allied land forces, aided by air support. Encounters between Japanese and American pilots resulted in destruction of two-thirds of the enemy's planes and most of their ships in the harbor. Ormoc was reduced to rubble and could no longer serve as a port of entry for Japanese troops and supplies.

A "last ditch" raid by the Japanese on airfields at Tacloban and Dulag was met and repelled. The 7-week struggle to occupy Leyte ended, but it would be followed by four months of cleaning out enemy pockets. A final casualty count of eighteen thousand for the Americans, including thirty-five hundred deaths, compared with an estimated loss of some seventy-five thousand for the Japanese with fewer than one thousand taken prisoner.

In November the Army Service Command opened Base K in Tacloban, and corpsmen and doctors were clearing sites, putting up prefab structures and tent frames, and laying floors without the help of the engineers, who were busy building airfields.

One month after the initial landing, most of the hospitals on Leyte still were not ready to receive the sick and wounded. Essential equipment, such as generators, X-ray machines, water purifiers, and microscopes, was held up by torrential rains and muddy footing. At that time the twenty-six nurses in the hospital at Palo were the only Army women on the island.

Meanwhile on Biak with its major hospital complex the morale of a group of rigorously trained flight nurses was shattered by the long delay. These nurses had to work at fatiguing lower altitudes of four to ten thousand feet to preserve warmth for severely wounded patients. The passengers were carried in C-47 or C-54 planes that were used for cargoes on outbound flights and hence not marked with a cross to show their identity as hospitals on their return.

The nurses on these planes were trained in aeromedical physiology, the use of oxygen equipment, and ways to relieve pain, prevent hemorrhage, treat shock, and handle neuropsychiatric cases. They learned survival techniques and were required to qualify on the pistol range.

The Biak group spent weeks waiting to be put to work while enlisted flight technicians on C-47s brought patients in from Leyte as early as the end of October. The run was considered "too dangerous" for the nurses.

On November 26th the first contingent of WACs arrived in Tacloban from New Guinea and were strafed on the airstrip as they landed. Though the flight nurses had by then been placed on partial runs to Peleliu in the Central Pacific, a secure base, they waited until mid-December to be assigned to the full round-trip run from Biak to Tacloban and back.

On November 25th the 133rd General Hospital reached Tacloban aboard four LSTs and was the first fixed hospital successfully set in place. Medical staff assembled the equipment with great speed on a site one mile south of Palo and immediately had four hundred beds under canvas with corpsmen caring for the wounded.

The influx of nurses was delayed more by a transportation backup than a veto by Army commanders. A group who came on the *Hope* on December 4th was the vanguard of shipments soon to follow. During the month the weather eased enough to permit the unloading of more transports in the gulf so that mobile and fixed hospitals that had been held for weeks in sodden bases moved to new sites, were assembled and reorganized. Staff was not far behind.

Hortense McKay left Hollandia the day after Christmas with nurses from her own and two other hospitals. Upon arrival she remembered their climbing down the side of a ship on rope nets under cover of darkness in a drenching rain. They found patients bedded down in tents in the mud. They were among almost six hundred nurses on duty on the island by the end of the month. Many of the women who had been on temporary duty were glad to rejoin their own hospital teams.

As for Nola, her circuitous inspection schedule extended from New Guinea to Leyte and back and included a look at nursing conditions on six hospital ships. Most of these ships were manned by the U.S. Navy, but Nola remembered one with a Dutch captain and crew where she was invited to dinner and enjoyed being waited on by a string of youthful servants bringing one dish after another.

Nola described Christmastime on the island. "I was there and visited some hospitals. Of course, we had nothing of any type of supplies.

The Pacific really took it — we got very few things that we needed. The nurses tried to trim up little shrubs as Christmas trees. They would take toilet paper and soak it in Mercurochrome, make it red and make little bows on trees. The patients would help, the ones that were up and around. They were always so solicitous of each other. They would help their fellow patients."

Part of Christmas Day the leading nurse spent with General Eichelberger and his staff. The officers had set up a tent for a party when an air raid signal sent everyone running outside and diving for foxholes. In the dark each person poured the contents of his or her bottle into a common punchbowl, then took a cupful on the way out to drink in the watery shelter.

MacArthur chose Christmas Day to declare Leyte secure. Krueger and his Sixth Army pulled out, heading for Luzon. He was replaced by Gen. Robert L. Eichelberger, who commanded the Eighth Army, newly arrived from the United States. His orders were to conduct "mopping up operations," which turned out to be a lengthy and thankless task.

The end of the year revealed only 40 percent of the hospital beds on Leyte equipped to receive casualties, but that ratio rose as the weather continued to permit supplies and personnel to move forward. Bases to the rear were lightening their medical loads: the pioneer base in Port Moresby had only a "clean-up squad," and the one in Milne Bay mostly served the local forces. Soon almost half of the thirty thousand hospital beds in New Guinea were vacant as patients were shipped to the States.

In mid-January, Hortense McKay and her group moved to their permanent station, the 126th General Hospital west of Palo. Here construction had been delayed by drainage problems, and the nurses found most of the beds on wet ground. Medical officers and crews were working hard to cut bamboo for new wards as patients poured in from temporary treatment sites. The 126th kept expanding and grew to 3,300 beds, the largest on Leyte. It even had three wards for Japanese prisoners.

Captain McKay was the chief nurse of this hospital, and she conferred with Colonel Forrest when she came for inspections and doubtless entertained her at dinner. McKay was concerned with the total functioning of her hospital, including care of the patients in the wards. She described the extent of their injuries as "shocking ... arms missing, legs missing, deep scalp injuries, deep chest injuries ... faces all but destroyed! Unbelievable suffering!"

In mid-January Colonel Forrest made the official move from New Guinea to Leyte with the intermediate echelon of General Denit's staff. She still had time to keep in touch with her friends. A colleague in the China-Burma-India theater received a letter from her later that month, saying that she "had landed safely and enjoyed the experience."

She recalled that "engineer General [Hugh J. "Pat"] Casey had a house, kind of a shack, built for me and the staff. It had four bedrooms in it." She shared it with a major as assistant director, a captain responsible for matters of personnel, and a WAC typist.

In Leyte she devoted herself to the usual administrative duties as hospitals filled with patients. She worked to balance staffing loads, deal with promotions, and find ways to handle health and supply problems. But she continued this routine only a few weeks "until we went into Manila for the liberation of the nurses in Santo Tomas."

# CHAPTER 8

# FULL CIRCLE

I n January 1945, President Roosevelt urged in his State of the Union message that plans be drawn for drafting nurses. In the SWPA region some twenty-nine hundred Army nurses were working at full capacity, and the reserve pool was completely exhausted. Casualties from the fighting continued to pour into hospitals in Leyte and New Guinea, and medical teams anticipated more bloodshed as the invasion of Luzon moved past the planning stage.

This was the largest campaign of the Pacific war, drawing on fighting units of five nations and two American theaters. Admiral Kinkaid led the Seventh Fleet with an Australian squadron. Gen. George C. Kenney commanded the U.S. Fifth and Thirteenth Air Forces, with Australian and Dutch air groups. General Krueger continued to lead the Sixth Army and General Eichelberger, the Eighth. The entire undertaking was supported by naval groups borrowed from Admiral Nimitz, along with elements of the British navy.

A major landing was scheduled for the harbor of Lingayen Gulf halfway up the west coast of Luzon. MacArthur chose this beachhead for its proximity to the best roads and railways of the island. These ran through central plains south to Manila, 120 miles away. U.S. troops were to take this territory on their sweep to the capital, establishing control over a major portion of the island.

In mid-December, to establish air support, the Seventh Fleet carried combat troops and engineers to the island of Mindoro, just south of Luzon. Two troop ships were hit by kamikazes, and a ferocious storm caused three destroyers to capsize, drowning more than seven hundred men. Still, meeting little Japanese resistance, the Americans took the island and engineers soon had two fighter air strips were in operation.

Meanwhile the high command took measures to deceive the enemy as to the landing site. Allied bombers struck at targets in southern Luzon, and Filipino guerrillas in that area intensified their activities. PT boats patrolled the coasts as far up as Manila Bay, and landing ships approached the southwestern beaches.

On January 3rd the real invasion began when a fleet of almost one thousand warships and three thousand landing craft set out from Leyte Gulf. The fleet was almost forty miles in length. The first group, under Adm. Jesse Oldendorf, led the way, sailing south through Surigao Strait, then west past the island of Mindanao, turning north along the coasts of Panay and Mindoro toward their destination in Luzon.

This force had the initial task of clearing mines, conducting underwater demolition, and bombarding the Lingayen shore defenses three days before the actual landing. All along the way, and once in the waters of the gulf, the ships ran a gauntlet of attacks from kamikaze pilots taking off from airfields on Luzon. The trip was a nightmare for the sailors, many of whom died in agonizing pain on their burning ships and were buried at sea with their fallen officers.

Three other naval groups that followed, two of them made up of troop ships, received further kamikaze hits but were able to stay on course. MacArthur, assigned to the cruiser *Boise*, watched harrowing scenes of destruction from the deck and barely escaped death himself. The ships of the combined fleet, slowed by frequent evasive actions to avoid attack, took six days to assemble in Lingayen Gulf.

On the morning of January 9th as the Allied naval bombardment lifted, men, supplies, trucks, and tanks began to unload as fast as ground could be prepared by the engineers. In the Sixth Army a heavy landing force of the infantry's I Corps and XIV Corps started to push south across a broad plain of flatlands, good roads, and fields of rice. Their orders were to take Manila with all possible speed.

General Yamashita had two hundred and sixty thousand forces on

Luzon, too weak in modern equipment and transport to face the U.S. Army in open combat. He fought a delaying action by concentrating his troops in the mountains of northern Luzon, in the hills overlooking Clark Field, and in the high ground east of Manila. As the Allied infantry moved south, fighting grew more intense when the men encountered Japanese soldiers attacking from caves in the hills and felt anew the enemy's tenacity in defensive warfare.

In twelve days the Americans progressed as far south as Tarlac, almost halfway to Manila. MacArthur had promised the American joint chiefs of staff that he would reach Manila within four weeks of landing on Luzon. He used a strategy of pitting the Sixth Army under Krueger, advancing south toward the city, against the Eighth Army under Eichelberger, advancing north from Nichols Field. The 11th Airborne Division was to take the airfield a few miles south of Manila and follow further orders.

When enemy resistance stalled the airborne division short of Nichols Field, MacArthur revised his plans. He chose two of the Sixth Army's best divisions to compete in crossing the city's boundaries. On January 30th he ordered the commander of the 1st Cavalry — "Go to Manila, go around the Nips." A mechanized task force of the 1st Cavalry Brigade, then at Lingayen Gulf, began to "race" the 37th Division which was already near Clark Field fifty miles from the city.

MacArthur feared that the Japanese, becoming more and more desperate, would retaliate against the Allied prisoners in their hands. The general was, in his own words, "deeply concerned about the thousands of prisoners who had been interned at the various camps on Luzon since the early days of the war — American, British and other Allied nationals, including women and children. I knew that many of these half-starved and ill-treated people would die unless we rescued them promptly."

In a separate action on January 30th more than five hundred weak and disabled inmates at the Cabanatuan military prison camp, some sixty miles northeast of Manila, were freed in a surprise encounter within enemy lines. Picked men from the Sixth Army's Ranger Battalion and a group of Filipino guerrillas stormed the camp, killed the guards, and saved all these remaining Bataan survivors.

Four days later, a flying column of eight hundred men from the 1st

Cavalry Division crossed the Manila city limits at dusk. Led around land mines in the darkened streets by a Filipino scout they headed for Santo Tomas University in a densely populated area.

⇥ ══✦══ ⇤

The history of the Santo Tomas Internment Camp was an epic of survival. It began in January 1942 when the Japanese occupied Manila. They canvassed the Allied citizens — British, American, Australian, Dutch, Canadian, and others — and told them to meet at specified locations with food and clothing for three days. They registered them as enemy aliens and took them to Santo Tomas University, which faced on Calle España in the heart of the city.

Founded in 1611 by monks of the Dominican Order, this old school was moved to the northeastern section of Manila in 1927, although its medical department remained within the Intramuros. The university's teaching mission was interrupted by the enemy occupation, and for the next three years the Japanese incarcerated more than seven thousand people on its 60-acre campus, although the total number usually did not exceed much more than four thousand.

The camp was put in charge of the Japanese military police, who took no responsibility for the care and feeding of their captives. By mid-January more than three thousand men, women, and children had poured into eight campus buildings where they tried to sleep in crowded classrooms without beds or mosquito nets. During the daytime they suffered further discomforts, one of which was persistent hunger. A number of them were also seriously ill.

Many people were saved by their faithful Filipino house servants and anxious friends and neighbors, who swarmed outside an iron picket fence in front of the main gate with food and clothing, bedding, furniture, and toiletries, which they passed through the fence. To control this flood, the camp command set up tables inside the grounds manned by Japanese guards, who inspected all packages for weapons, flashlights, liquor, or notes, which had to be censored.

Some internees had been staff members of the Philippine Red Cross, and they were able to help the people form a community. Through colleagues in Manila they procured beds, kitchenware and dining utensils, foodstuffs, medicines, surgical and hospital equipment, building materials, plumbing, and electrical supplies. In this way they set up a mass feeding system and treated hundreds of sick internees in improvised hospitals.

A bureaucracy was soon established. Three former corporate executives formed the core of a central committee, which negotiated with the Japanese command and supervised a budding structure of subcommittees. These drew on talents in many fields and set up working schedules. People who volunteered as room monitors, cleaning crews, kitchen help, and carpenters found themselves given regular duties.

A labor pool of one thousand men provided construction workers, plumbers, and engineers, as well as a large crew to build a three-acre vegetable garden from a former dump. Male volunteers installed toilets and more than fifty shower baths. Sanitation teams fought an endless battle against flies, mosquitoes, and rodents. Women mended mosquito nets and made aprons, sheets and pillow slips. Other people picked maggots out of the food.

To keep the children occupied, internees established classes. Soon adults signed up for their own classes in Spanish, French, Latin, art, geometry, chemistry, astronomy, engineering, typing, and shorthand.

Clergymen and missionaries held services, and an entertainment committee put on a vaudeville show as early as the end of January. Athletic teams — softball, basketball, and soccer — sought members and organized games. One man brought in broadcasting equipment and played popular songs from a large supply of donated records.

By mid-summer the Japanese decided to assume responsibility for camp costs, providing a sum of thirty-five cents per person per day from which the people bought food, sanitation supplies, and fuel. Since this allowance was far from enough to meet every need, the leaders tapped the internee community for supplementary funds.

The captives were under constant pressure from the frustrating rules and regulations imposed by the Japanese. Men with wives who were citizens of Allied countries brought their families with them, and forty-five babies were born the first year. But married men and women had to sleep separately in the university buildings in densely packed quarters.

Many male blue-collar workers from Allied countries who were civilian employees of the naval yard or miners and dock hands were married to Filipinas. Since their wives were not considered enemy aliens, they had to remain outside with the children. All the single males were jammed into classrooms or in a crowded dormitory in the gymnasium, which soon became malodorous in the oppressive heat and filled with rats.

Some families with money sought relief from the crowding by building open-sided shanties on the grounds near the walls, purchasing materials through friends outside or from funds that were smuggled in. Here they could join each other in the daytime and talk more freely. As many as six hundred shanties were built, divided into "towns" with street names and unofficial mayors.

By July 1942, despite serious deprivations, a cohesive community was already functioning with clear lines of authority. At this point the Japanese brought in fifty-five Army nurses from Corregidor, not knowing where else to put them. These women had served earlier that year near the fighting as the USAFFE forces struggled to hold off the enemy in southern Luzon.

Using rapidly depleted medical supplies, living on short rations and working long hours in heavy tropical heat, nurses in two jungle hospitals on the Bataan peninsula provided care for sick and wounded soldiers. Casualties from nearby combat poured into the hospitals where two men often shared one bed with no mosquito nets and some patients lay on the ground. The poorly supplied troops, having eaten anything they could find in the jungle, became infected with a host of tropical diseases and parasites that weakened their ability to heal. For their diet a nurse described how she doled out a stew of mule or carabao or even monkey with fish, rice and some green weeds. Soon the meals for everyone consisted mostly of rice.

Late in March the Japanese started bombing one of the hospitals despite its Red Cross marking, killing some of the patients and wounding two of the nurses. The situation on the fighting front became so desperate that on April 8th General Wainwright ordered all the nurses to the island of Corregidor and withdrew to the island himself. The nurses were deeply upset to leave hundreds of sick and wounded men under their care lying in cots in the open air; they had no choice. The next day Bataan fell to the enemy.

The nurses from Bataan joined their colleagues on duty in the

Malinta Tunnel hospital on The Rock. Waves of wounded men filled the hospital wings where the beds were triple-decked. The doctors and nurses worked in choking dust during bombings and labored in darkness when the generators failed. The air was infested with black flies, roaches, and mosquitoes. The stench of bodies, septic wounds, and gas gangrene suffocated caregivers and patients.

Members of the medical staff were crammed with military personnel in the underground corridors of the fortress where they endured days and nights of artillery pounding and bombing from the air. During the siege the nurses, living on two meager meals a day and getting little sleep, acquired coughs from the polluted air and fungus infections from the dampness. They developed fevers and chronic disorders. At the end of April and the first few days in May, General Wainwright evacuated thirty-one of them to Australia. Some were older or seriously rundown, and others were chosen inexplicably. A few on the initial list refused to go.

On May 6th, Wainwright was forced to surrender the fort. Food and medical supplies were almost gone. The hospital contained about nine hundred patients, many severely wounded. The nurses and the rest of the medical staff, after submitting to long interrogations from their captors, were permitted to care for their patients under the supervision of the enemy. The women were not molested, but all their possessions — rings, watches, jewelry, radios, pens, and cigarette lighters — were stolen. They had to bow from the waist every time a Japanese officer appeared.

Two months later the Japanese commandant ordered the Corregidor hospital moved to Manila. By this time nearly all of the Army nurses were suffering from serious effects of physical deprivation. On July 2nd they climbed with their failing strength aboard an old freighter, the *Lima Maru*, for a trip across Manila Bay with their patients and the doctors, corpsmen, and Filipina nurses with whom they had worked.

Once ashore, they felt sadness on separating from these people who had so bravely shared their ordeal. They watched them as they were driven away to Old Bilibid prison while they themselves were taken elsewhere.

Back home news reached ANC headquarters in Washington, D.C., of the fate of the Corregidor nurses. As Nola Forrest fulfilled her endless duties on the home front, she kept pushing for an overseas assignment, "particularly to the Pacific area [where] many of my good friends were prisoners of the Japanese."

Taken to the Santo Tomas Internment Camp, her friends were registered, their baggage was inspected, and the entire group was shunted to the two-story Santa Catalina convent and school dormitory across the street from the campus. The Japanese were keeping them incommunicado to suppress any news of atrocities. The women were suffering from arthritis, hepatitis, leg ulcers, tropical fevers, and dysentery, aside from deep exhaustion. For almost seven weeks they slept, ate, and healed under the care of a camp doctor and had their first real opportunity to get acquainted with each other.

The camp commndant permitted one contact with a friend from outside, Mrs. Ida Hentsche Hube, who appeared as though from heaven. An early member of the Army Nurse Corps, she had resigned in 1910 upon her marriage to a prosperous importer whom she met while serving in Manila. At the time of the Japanese occupation she was living in the plush Manila Hotel, and as the widow of a German and herself German-born, she was not interned.

Allowed to speak with two of her former colleagues at the door of the convent, she was shocked at their gaunt appearance. She immediately sent the entire group quantities of fresh fruits, cakes, canned milk, sewing kits, and clothes, delivered in her limousine. For many months her Filipino servants would bring bundles of food, sanitary napkins, needles, thread, yarn, and money twice a week to the package line in two pushcarts.

In August the executive committee convinced the Japanese commandant that the camp hospital needed more room and that the Santa Catalina convent, which had more space, was the best place to put it. They argued that the Army nurses should join the hospital's nursing staff. The day the nurses moved into the main camp Mrs. Hube sent six roasted pigs for a celebration.

Capt. Maude Davison, their leader, was determined to keep them together, and she organized them into a corps. They were given khaki skirts and white shirts, and they worked at the hospital in 4-hour day shifts and 8-hour night shifts throughout their stay. The hospital had seventy-five beds, an American medical director, assisted by several medical missionaries, and a Manila physician. A clinic on the first floor served outpatients. The nurses were sternly supervised by Captain Davison, who had a room on the upper floor for her quarters and office. First Lieutenant Josephine Nesbit shared her task.

A lively history of the nurses' stay in Santo Tomas was written by Denny Williams, a married former Army nurse whose husband was called up when the Japanese attacked and who had volunteered her services. She described the scene when she and her friends were finally allowed to enter the plaza in front of the Main Building as "like a country fair, a carnival inside a pressure cooker. Hordes of people mingled freely, crowding around a market to buy fresh fruits or vegetables, and surrounding numerous vendors ... Everyone talked a mile a minute as if no Japanese lurked just around the corner."

The Japanese commandants were frequently replaced, but all of them subjected the community to arbitrary rules. Under the control of their superiors they administered  policies on grants of freedom and the movements of groups in and out of the camp. The inmates, despite the indignities forced upon them, were determined not to be humiliated. They tried to "keep face" by acting cheerful and unconcerned in spite of universal crowding, hunger pangs, common showers, and long waits in line to use the toilet.

A loudspeaker awakened everyone at 6:30 a.m., and people stood in a chow line for mush, a banana, some coconut milk, and a little brown sugar and water. At first some meat was included in meals, but toward the end of 1943 five o'clock supper consisted of vegetable stew over rice, a slice of bread, a banana, and "tea." Bedtime was at 9:00 p.m. when the loudspeaker played "Goodnight, Ladies."

As for the nurses, Denny described the way they spent their free time — scrounging for food, washing clothes, taking showers, taking naps, playing bridge, or attending classes in the evening. The days were heavy with ennui, and conversation often lagged. Denny wrote a paper for her English class, entitled "How to Attract Bores and Waste Time in Santo Tomas."

At first the Japanese let the medical teams run their own activities and permitted critically ill patients and women about to deliver their babies to be sent to existing hospitals in Manila. The internees themselves organized three additional outside hospitals for the elderly, convalescents, and children. Some sick internees were even released.

In September 1942 ten more Army nurses arrived in Santo Tomas. They had been among those flown out during the last days before Corregidor fell. Their rescue plane was disabled upon landing on Mindanao, and they were captured a few days later. After first working in a Philippine hospital, they were placed in two different camps by the Japanese before joining their colleagues in Manila.

There they fitted into the routine and soon found themselves thinking about food like everyone else. At Christmas, however, a special treat in the form of a plentiful dinner came for Denny and her friends from Mrs. Hube and the Filipina Nurses Association. More than seven hundred visitors were allowed into camp, and the Philippine Bureau of Mines brought four roasted pigs to their three hundred interned employees.

Men and women made toys — tiny trains, jigsaw puzzles, boats, and dolls — for the 435 children under twelve, and Santa delivered two thousand wrapped gifts. The Japanese sent photographers to record the humane treatment they were providing their captives.

Behind the scenes were some grim realities. In February two Britishers and an Australian had escaped over the wall, and they were caught as they tried to get away. Brought back, they were severely beaten, moved out, and condemned to death. They were taken to the Chinese cemetery where they were shot and pushed into an open grave, still moaning.

Marie Adams, a Red Cross field director held with the other internees, was put in charge of medical statistics, abstracts, and birth and death certificates, and she later testified to the U.S. War Crimes Office on the condition of people brought into the camp hospital from the dungeon in Fort Santiago. They evidenced severe malnutrition, dysentery and beriberi, infestation by vermin, and sometimes festering wounds. Many bore marks of torture and emotional disturbance.

One of them was Frederic Stevens, who had headed a Manila group that was making plans before the war against a Japanese attack. Removed from the camp, he was imprisoned in the fort with two Manila newspaper editors. For eight months the three men had to sit up all day and lie on the cold floor all night in a crowded cell amid lice, bedbugs, cockroaches, and mosquitoes. They were fed very little, were beaten and tortured. Near the point of collapse they were released to the camp hospital.

In May 1943 the Japanese sent 787 male internees and eleven Navy nurses, at their request, to a new internment camp at Los Baños, the site of an agricultural college, about forty miles away on the shores of Laguna de Bay. Some of the doctors went with them. This move caused a shortage of men for hard physical labor at Santo Tomas even as more than eight hundred additional internees were brought in, many old and ill, and a number with small children.

Marie Adams told how the Philippine Red Cross sent supplies of drugs and medicines and gave vaccinations against cholera and typhoid. Further drugs and medical needs, though never enough, were purchased from outside, and a windfall of relief supplies came in October 1943 via the M.S. *Gripsholm*, a diplomatic exchange ship that took 127 prisoners home.

At Christmas that year a community chorus of the internees performed Handel's *Messiah*, and a movie was shown. But no visitors were allowed in the camp, and Christmas dinner consisted of stinking fish. At day's end the loudspeaker played "I Got Plenty of Nothin'. "

In 1944, as the fortunes of war were shifting in favor of the Allies, living conditions worsened. In February the military police of the Imperial Japanese Army took charge of the camp, and they cut the food supply. Cash per diems were canceled; the authorities would now supply the camp with meals; they would no longer permit purchases in Manila markets. They closed the package line at the fence although Ida Hube managed more than once to smuggle in money and precious food. Within two months the command reduced the average daily diet to rice or corn, foul-tasting fish, and sometimes sweet potatoes and coconut milk.

"At night in dreams," wrote Denny, "I kept going off on food binges. But every time I approached a table loaded with hamburgers and milkshakes, someone pulled me away. Although I tugged, I could never get free and eat my fill. Invariably I awoke to a flourish of trumpets and a harsh voice saying, 'Your attention please' ... words that made us cringe."

In March the camp command held a practice air raid drill was held, the first of many. They ordered a barbed wire fence to be built on top of the wall surrounding the campus and a higher bamboo fence outside. Large groups of people were shifted in and out of the camp as the military outlook changed.

That spring infectious diseases spread among children and adults, and the increase in tuberculosis cases called for a new isolation hospital in one of the buildings. The medical staff, cut off from contact with out-side physicians or hospitals, were forced to cope with containment of epidemics and with critically dwindling stocks of drugs and equipment. They had to handle obstetrical cases, surgery, acute illnesses, and deaths. By May 1944 two hundred people in the camp had died.

In mid-summer the guards became suspicious during a minstrel show when the crowd laughed hilariously as a quartet sang:

> The rumors give us lots of hope,
> It's amazing what you hear.
> According to the latest dope
> We were all set free last year.

The commandant demanded a look at the script, ordered an apol-ogy, and further entertainment was forbidden.

By summer all money in the camp had to be surrendered; each individual could keep only fifty pesos. Colonel Toshio Hayashi described as "inhuman and cruel," took charge as chief officer. Male internees were punished for minor infractions, sometimes forced to stand for hours outside the front gate in the broiling sun. Bowing rules for everyone were strictly enforced.

Yet the command could not suppress the shouts of joy that spread through the camp on September 21st as more than one hundred U.S. planes flew over Manila for the first time, diving, bombing, and strafing. A chilling voice over the loudspeaker soon announced that anyone look-ing out the windows would be shot. Hopes fell when Allied troops did not appear, even though the air raids continued throughout the fall and just before Christmas the first B-29 Superfortresses passed slowly overhead.

By this time people were beginning to die of starvation as the food ration was further decreased. In December twenty-three deaths occurred, and in January, thirty-two. The daily menu consisted of a few spoonfuls of rice for breakfast, boiled greens for lunch, and rice or corn mush with beans for dinner. People were eating cats, dogs, pigeons, and canna bulbs.

Because of the low caloric intake maintenance teams could no longer do their jobs. Eyes were dull, skin was like parchment, and many found their feet so swollen they could barely walk. A shortage of water eliminated laundry, and low pressure disabled most of the toilets. Since each person had been issued just one cake of soap every two months and no toilet paper for a year, the poor state of personal hygiene added to the suffering.

The enemy was growing more and more vindictive as rumors of random arrests in the city spread throughout the camp. The commandant ordered a list of all male internees between eighteen and fifty years of age, and people feared that the Japanese might massacre everyone before help could arrive.

Finally, at dawn on February 3rd a boom was heard. Planes flew over the camp, and one pilot dropped his goggles with a message that said "Roll out the barrel!" After supper the people heard a rumble getting louder. As the sun was setting, the loudspeaker ordered them inside. The lights went out.

At 9:00 p.m. a crash at the front gate and the lumbering sounds of tanks were followed for a moment by silence. An American voice rang through the darkness, then some shots. The glare of a searchlight revealed enemy soldiers fleeing inside as scores of starving people swarmed onto the plaza with cries of joy and rushed to embrace their rescuers.

The American troops could not fire on the Japanese guards in the midst of the crowd. The guards dashed into the Education Building where Colonel Hayashi was holding more than two hundred inmates hostage and refused to leave. For forty-eight hours tense negotiations continued between interpreters on both sides while intermittent cross-fire breached the walls and wounded a few men outdoors in the dark. Finally the enemy was given safe conduct out of the camp, and only then could the captive people celebrate their liberation in front of the Main Building as they cheered the unfurling of the Stars and Stripes.

During the hostage crisis the American soldiers set up tents on the grounds and built fires. They opened their own food cans and gave away their rations. Supply trucks from Lingayen soon poured into the campus with food and medical items along with vitamins, bedding, and pajamas. The Red Cross brought four thousand letters from relatives and friends, and an officer from the Transportation Corps came from Leyte to assume command.

On February 7th, General MacArthur entered Manila and first went to visit the eight hundred sick and starving military prisoners at Old Bilibid prison, the remnants of his former USAFFE command. Many of them were too weak to recognize him, and some could speak only in whispers.

He then proceeded to Santo Tomas Internment Camp where the response was overwhelming. "The welcome was hysterical as he was thoroughly surrounded by happy, shouting, talking, weeping people," wrote his doctor. "He couldn't move." The throng included most of the nurses from Bataan and Corregidor, as well as business leaders he had known in Manila before the war.

<hr />

As patients began to arrive in Leyte hospitals from the fighting in Luzon, Maj. Mary Parker, the chief nurse in Base K, was struggling to establish routine medical operations. The base was at the end of a 6000-mile supply line, making for bottlenecks in ship unloadings. The terrain consisted of swamps and rice paddies, and hospitals were deep in the mud. The climate was stifling, and enemy nuisance raids added to the stress.

In December, when the Army nurses first came, "Food was barely edible, water was barely potable, and no laundry service was available," wrote Forrest and Brady in their later report. The nurses washed their clothes in their helmets. They were quartered in prefab buildings, holding twelve, or in pyramidal tents for four. They slept under mosquito nets on Army cots. Eventually the Seabees made them floors and screens and even provided electric lights. But their quarters were guarded, and they had little time for recreation.

In January when Colonel Forrest reached her new station on Leyte, she focused her attention on staff problems in the hospitals on the island. She was fully occupied when she was ordered on February 8th to fly to Luzon with one hundred  nurses and twenty doctors "to direct the nursing service in the forward area and to supervise care of nurses recently liberated from POW status." Her group had been gathered from hospitals in rear areas and augmented by some new arrivals from the States. Her assistant was Maj. Helen Gray.

"We flew in," Nola recounted. "I think there were probably three planes, and we got in [to Clark Field] about eight o'clock in the evening. They had torn-up jeeps along the runways with their lights on so we knew where to land. Then the next morning we were all to go down to Santo Tomas, a ride of about forty miles from San Juan, which was near Clark Air Force Base. I think they put tents up that night.

"We just got in, and the surgeon who was in charge of the medical unit there said to me, 'You know, they tell me that the medical commander of the Sixth Army is about ten miles from here, and we should go there and report — don't you think so?' I said all right, though I was ready for bed. So we get in this jeep, and we have a driver, and we have two men with rifles, and we start that trip, and we are in Jap territory most of the time. But we get there, and we see the colonel and report, and he tells us what we can expect when we get to Manila. He hadn't been there yet.

"Well, as we came back, there was a raid on. The Jap bombers were above us, and we were on this highway that was raised up high ... you could look down one side probably thirty or forty feet to what seemed to be a river below. We were going along, and the driver says, 'I'm going to turn the lights off.' And I said to the colonel, 'Oh, we can't do that. I'd rather take a chance from the bombers than I would going over the cliff.' So we talked to the driver, and I said, 'Wouldn't you be going fast enough that it would be pretty hard to hit us from up there?'

"We got back to San Juan about three in the morning. Then, about five thirty they handed us some coffee and a piece of hard cracker, and we all got in trucks and had to stand up in those trucks for forty miles. We got down to Santo Tomas, and this was two days after MacArthur had come in and visited them, and they were all just terribly excited."

Right after MacArthur's visit, the Japanese began shelling the compound. They delivered three bombardments that day, and the Main Building took a direct hit. Here an emergency ward and operating room had been set up to treat internees and soldiers wounded during the hostage crisis. The interned Army nurses, despite their weakened condition, rushed in to care for the casualties.

The 893rd Medical Clearing Company reached the camp from Lingayan Gulf and opened a hospital in the Education Building. With them came an 8-man kitchen crew, who started to feed hundreds of ravenous captives even as the hospital filled up with one hundred patients from the camp and the fighting in the streets outside. Heavy shelling continued for the next five days, raising the patient load to one hundred and fifty.

"Dead, dying, and wounded internees and soldiers poured into emergency on stretchers carried by internee volunteers," wrote Denny Williams. "We worked all through the first night of shelling, and ... we slept on blankets on the floor whenever we could grab a few minutes."

On February 9th during a lull in the fighting Nola Forrest's group appeared with reinforcements. The convoy drew up at the Santa Catalina dormitory while patients were being moved over to the campus to make room for the new medical team. Nola recalled the brilliance of the fires raging in the city, the towers of black smoke, and the pounding of the Japanese artillery.

"We had sixty-seven nurses, Army nurses, who had been prisoners in there for almost three years, and two of them were very special friends of mine," Nola explained. Unlike the rest of the internees the nurses, as military officers, were prisoners of war. Two nurses from Baguio, captured at Camp John Hay in the mountains northeast of Lingayen Gulf, had joined their number. One was sent to Santo Tomas in 1943, and the other was brought over from Old Bilibid Prison just after the rescue.

Nola felt a mixture of disbelief and joy as she recognized the faces of old friends — among them Mina Aasen, Eleanor O'Neill, and Josie Nesbit — and as she met Denny Williams, whom she had heard of, and many more. She greeted civilian women with whom she had served in Manila back in the twenties, nurses who had married their suitors and stayed in the Philippines.

Not overlooking the pleasure of gifts, Nola stocked up before leaving Leyte on anything she could find. "I went to the PX, and I got a lot of candy bars, and I had saved up some liquor and some jewelry — we couldn't wear it anyhow, some earrings and stuff — so I had those fixed up for these people. I gave these to this friend of mine. But I didn't give her the candy at first. 'Oh,' she said, 'I'd give just anything for a bar of candy.' 'Well,' I said, 'I've got a bar of candy, too.'

"When we came in, of course, those nurses were so happy. They had had to take care of the people in there most of the time, and they were worn out. People said that within two months everybody would have starved to death because the Japanese knew this was coming, and they kept reducing their rations. Everybody had a tin can, and they said you could just hear that tin can going with all trying to get every last morsel out of it. I think they were given rice that they said had maggots in it and a vegetable on the order of spinach. That's about all they got to eat. They were terribly weak. They'd all lost weight." She also noted the pallor of their faces, contrasting with the yellow skin of their rescuers with bloodstreams full of Atabrine.

The camp's mimeographed *Liberation Bulletin*, dated February 3rd, 1945, contained eight pages of detailed information about the camp and mock advertisements for Manila business firms. One item was a table showing the average loss of weight among the adults. From 1942 until August 15, 1944 the men each lost 27 pounds, and the women 16 pounds. Then, in just five months, from August 15, 1944 until January 20, 1945, the men lost another 24 pounds, the women another 16 pounds.

"The first couple of days we were there," said Nola, "we were housed in a convent, Santa Catalina, that was connected to the hospital, and told to be very careful not to go out, there were so many Jap snipers around. We slept there at night.

"In the camp I saw where the nurses lived. They had maybe eight in a room, and they did have beds. But they never knew, day or night, when the Japanese would come round and search. They were told they'd be killed if they had any money on them, but some of them kept pesos all that time. Otherwise, the Japanese didn't molest them. Of course, they always had to bow very low every time a Japanese officer came by. Everybody in the camp did that. Only thing, after American planes started flying over, if they looked up at the sky, then the Japanese made them look at the sun for a while.

"After we came in," Nola went on, "the irony was that Santo Tomas was caught in a crossfire between the Japanese and the American troops. It destroyed part of one whole building. I can remember being on the floor of the Red Cross hut. This friend of mine was married to a businessman in Manila, but during the Santo Tomas days he was in charge of the Red Cross in the camp, so he had this little hut. There were about eight of us in there that night of the shelling."

The medical clearing company, reinforced by the new hospital team, continued to administer care under fire as casualties mounted. By the end of the engagement, nearly three hundred people had been hit. Nineteen internees were killed, and more than ninety were seriously injured. One of the nurses was hit but recovered. A rescued nurse later wrote, "To see the torn bodies of people who had waited for this day for so long, only to die or be maimed when their freedom was so close, was almost unbearable."

Nola and all the nurses in her group were later awarded the Bronze Star medal for their devoted care to the besieged people. The citation read: "For heroic achievement in Luzon ... from 9 February 1945 to 24 February 1945 ... these officers of the Army Nurse Corps were ordered into a bitterly contested combat zone to provide medical care for ... civilians suffering from malnutrition and other maladies resulting from long internment ... Despite air raids, artillery and small arms fire which inflicted casualties among patients and military person-nel ... they strove long and successfully to conserve lives endangered by enemy action. By their high courage, zeal, and selfless devotion to duty these officers rendered a valuable service in a period of extreme emer-gency during the Luzon campaign."

In less than three weeks the 893rd Medical Clearing Company departed with their cook, who had served countless meals and was said to be the "best cook in the Army. Even when the buildings were rock-ing from gunfire he managed to bake cake for the whole hospital." The emergency medical group also left the camp and was replaced by the 5th Field Hospital. By then the Army nurses who had survived captivi-ty were landing in California.

Colonel Forrest had moved swiftly to get all of them out of Manila. "We were trying to get the nurses back to the States as soon as possible," she recalled. "An Army officer who was in charge of all the transportation — he'd been a big businessman in Manila — came to me, and he said, 'I have the first plane that's coming into Manila ... and I'll give it to you for the nurses if they can get off the ground within thirty minutes.' Of course, they had very little luggage, and none of them weighed very much."

In the midst of the confusion, the American officer in charge of the camp came to Nola with a problem. "It seemed two of the people wanted to get married. They came and wanted to know, and he said, 'I don't know what we can do about this. I'll sign my name if you'll sign yours,' and I said yes, and we signed the licenses that gave them permission."

The couple were Bertha Dworsky, one of the nurses, and John Henderson, a civilian. They were married in the university museum chapel the night before the nurses' departure, and the groom was left behind. Later on, six other nurses, including Josie Nesbit, married men they had known in the camp.

In Denny Williams's history, "Colonel Forrest passed the word for us to be ready to leave the next morning [February 12th]. She said she would accompany us to Leyte where intelligence officers wanted to debrief us. 'You're the first women to have served under actual combat conditions,' she explained, a trace of emotion in her voice as if she would like to have been with us ... 'whatever tips you have on how you survived could be of great help to other women if the same situation ever arises.'

"She went on to say we would be given a promotion ... and that Roosevelt had ordered the Presidential Citation with two oak leaf clusters and a Bronze Star Medal for each of us ... The next morning we stood our last roll call in the Plaza, 67 nurses, plus a Red Cross Field Director, two dietitians, and a physical therapist ... I felt no grief on leaving Santo Tomas."

"When we knew the nurses were going back," Nola continued, "we had to equip them with uniforms, they had no clothes. So [Capt. Chadbourne] in my office flew over to New Guinea where there was a quartermaster depot of sorts, took all the dress and shoe sizes of these people, saw everything packed in boxes and flew back [to Leyte] with her load. It was quite a job, long trips each way. I don't imagine the uniforms fit too well, and they were pretty hot on the day that they left for home.

"When the plane came down, it was a C-46, a much smaller plane than I had expected, to take their belongings and them and everything. But anyhow we got them all on. I even squeezed in Denny Williams, who was a former member of the Army Nurse Corps imprisoned with the others because she had served on Corregidor. I got on the plane with them, and as we started over, almost to Mindoro, I heard an engine conk out. These were only 2-motor planes, cargo planes. I went up to the pilot, and he said, 'I think I can make Mindoro.' And we did. Then I went up to Operations, and they gave me two other planes to get the rest of the way to Leyte."

There the nurses were taken to the 126th General Hospital where Hortense McKay told how she scrounged enough beds and how nurses from all the local hospitals gave the ex-POWs their best nylon bras, nightgowns, soap, and personal effects. Emotions were running high.

"In Leyte," Nola recalled, "they had set up tents, and the Air Force had made up many extra batches of ice cream for the nurses. People were working all night long to get the orders written for promotions and Bronze Stars and their evacuation to the States. We had no first lieutenant's bars, but they nearly all had second lieutenant's bars. So we dipped those gold bars in mercury [to look like silver], and we had them ready. Two or three of them made captain. [Several days later] they were all marched out and given their promotion orders. Then we sent them on their way."

According to a joint account of the group in the May 1945 issue of *The American Journal of Nursing*, "When we landed at the Tacloban Air Strip...we had a difficult time trying to keep our feet on the ground. Some of our girls were hospitalized. The rest of us were billeted in a convalescent hospital set up on a wide, spacious beach ... We were fed continually. We rested; were fed; were interviewed and photographed, were fed again.

"A few days before we left, our summer uniforms were issued to us with shoes and rayon stockings. We had never worn this ANC uniform before ... We strutted and primped, bemoaning our loss of weight. For three years we had worn the same shirts and skirts made by the Quartermaster on the Rock supplemented by a few extra pieces, but our interest in clothes was stimulated mighty rapidly....

"Just before our departure from Leyte, we were thrilled by the award of the Bronze Star to each of us and also a promotion in rank. Even while General Guy B. Denit, the Chief Surgeon of the SWPA, presented the awards, we felt that it could not be really happening."

Most of the nurses were put on big Pan Am planes and flown to Hawaii and then on to the States. They enjoyed a delicious lunch en route, prepared by the base unit of the Air Transport Command. The menu consisted of three kinds of sandwiches — turkey, minced ham or deviled cheese — a hard boiled egg, olives, cake with chocolate icing, chilled pineapple, and coffee.

A smaller group returned on an airevac plane — those nurses, according to Nola, "that weren't quite as well, NP [neuropsychiatric], and the chief nurse that had been there. She had been quite sick, and she was elderly." Capt. Maude Davison weighed eighty pounds when she was rescued. In 1946 she was awarded the Legion of Merit.

The first leg of the Pan Am flight took the nurses to Honolulu, and the second leg brought them into Hamilton Field in California. A news photograph showed them dancing with joy as they touched home soil. According to Nola, "They had a wonderful welcome in San Francisco. You ever heard of Omar Khayyam's? Mardikian called them the Angels of Bataan. He entertained them at his home and put on a big feast for them at his restaurant."

Soon after Nola had returned to her permanent station, Surgeon General Norman T. Kirk arrived at the Tacloban base. MacArthur would not allow him in the combat zone, presumably because of the danger. Kirk stormed, "My chief nurse can go to Manila, but I can't go." To mollify him, the nurses gave him a party.

Throughout the month of February, the fight for Manila raged on. As American troops encircled the city, a task force of glider infantry, parachutists, guerrillas, and supporting artillery made a daring rescue of the almost 2,150 internees, including the eleven Navy nurses, at the Los Banos Internment Camp. The captives were loaded onto water craft and ferried across the bay. That was on February 24th, and two days later they were being cared for in an evacuation hospital set up in New Bilibid Prison fifteen miles south of the city.

Military orders kept most of the remaining internees at Santo Tomas inside the walls, unaware of the horrors inflicted on the citizens outside. They were celebrating hysterically and for some of the younger women, making love with the soldiers. In March, however, when the city was secure, administrators declared they would have to leave for home or accept offers of repatriation.

By then an exodus of almost 360 had already taken place, and three thousand left for the United States in April. Even as departures continued, some internees found the process of relocation so difficult they were still looking for homes when the camp closed on the 14th of July.

Internees of the Santo Tomas
Internment Camp, Manila, Luzon,
cheer their liberation, February 6,
1945 (National Archives)

Army Nurse POWs
leave Santo Tomas
en route home,
February 12, 1945
(National Archives)

Manila street after battle
(National Archives)

Brig. Gen. Guy B. Denit awards the Bronze Star and promotions to former nurse POWs before their departure from Leyte, February 19, 1945 (National Archives)

Lt. Col. Nola Forrest with Maj. Gen Hugh Wilde, commander Air Transport Group, and Capt. Josephine Nesbit, departing nurse leader, February 20, 1945 (National Archives)

Former nurse POWs in plane awaiting takeoff from Tacloban, Leyte, February 20, 1945 (National Archives)

Maj. Gen. Norman T. Kirk, Army surgeon general, and Maj. Pauline Kirby, Hollandia, New Guinea, February 15, 1945 (National Archives)

CHAPTER 9

# REENTRY

Once the nurse POWs were winging their way toward home, Nola Forrest returned her attention to administrative problems in Leyte hospitals where twenty thousand casualties from the fighting on Luzon would arrive in the first two months of the new year. One of her periodic reports for Control Section, dated February 15, 1945, turned up in the archives of the Army Nurse Corps Historian, providing a glimpse of her activities for one week.

The first paragraph of this 3-page, typewritten document mentions the promotions of the liberated nurses, their receipt of the Bronze Star award, and their departure for home. The rest focuses on the wearing of skirts versus slacks in various bases, training and employment of Filipina nurses' aides, and health programs for the nurses; also the handling of news stories on nurse POWs, transfers of nurses to Luzon, numbers of nurses versus patient requirements in each base, and nurse promotions in the theater.

Nola was working 10- to 12-hour days despite growing exhaustion and the onset of a mysterious soreness in the muscles of her left arm. In mid-March she moved with USASOS headquarters to Manila as the city came under U.S. control. Her medical group found space on the south side of the Pasig River in the center of a burnt-out area.

They came not long after a desperate struggle had taken place in the streets and buildings of the industrial area just south of the river. Enemy resistance was far greater than expected. MacArthur had hoped to stage a victory parade by mid-February, but as the month began, he found the battle for Manila would call for a powerful effort. Units of the U.S. 37th Division that had moved to a position on the south bank of the river on February 7th faced withering mortar, machine-gun, and rifle fire as their men moved westward toward the official buildings of the capital.

General Yamashita had moved his soldiers out of Manila according to his plan to hold Luzon against the Allies in the hills and surrounding ground in a delaying action, leaving the city virtually defenseless. But Adm. Sanji Iwabuchi, in command of sixteen thousand naval troops, maintained that Manila should be defended to the bitter end. He fought tenaciously, augmenting his forces with almost four thousand Japanese army troops that were caught in the city when the U.S. Army entered sooner than expected.

Iwabuchi ordered the demolition of all the city's military installations — the port area, all the bridges, the municipal water supply, and the electric power system. Streets were barricaded and sown with mines; buildings were booby-trapped.

As the U.S. infantry moved toward the west of the city, the 1st Cavalry pushed its way up Dewey Boulevard along Manila Bay, fighting die-hard enemy defenders for the Army Navy Club, the Manila Hotel, the Philippine general hospital, and the University of the Philippines.

By February 22nd, Iwabuchi's surviving troops were cornered in an area in the west of the city south of the Pasig. This contained the Intramuros, the ancient walled Spanish fortress. The last stages of this battle were fought there where the enemy was holding some four thousand Filipinos hostage. After six days of heavy bombardment by U.S. artillery, the Japanese released three thousand frightened civilians, mostly women and children. When the battle ended, the male hostages were found to have been executed and their bodies piled in the dungeons.

The fight for the heart of Manila was vicious, involving room-to-room and hand-to-hand combat in the government buildings and inside the Walled City. Not until March 3rd could Lt. Gen. Oscar Griswold, commander of the XIV Corps, report to Krueger that the last organized resistance had ceased.

Elements of the Sixth and Eighth armies had gained control of Nichols Field and Fort McKinley, south and southeast of the city's boundaries, respectively, helping to drive Iwabuchi from his headquarters in Fort McKinley into the Intramuros. By the time Nola arrived in Manila, the outskirts of the city were secure. She remembered taking a sightseeing tour.

"One of the doctors said to me, I'd known him a long time, his father had been surgeon general, 'I think I can get a jeep this afternoon. If I can, would you like to drive out to see Fort McKinley?' This was Col. [Paul] Ireland. He was born at Fort McKinley when his father was a surgeon there years before. So I said, 'Well, I certainly would.' So we did, but there was nothing there. It was absolutely obliterated. When we came back — we got halfway back, and the guards all stopped us — the colonel said, 'What's the matter?' The guard said, 'This road is heavily mined.'

"The guard showed us where to get over to a safe distance. It was on the Escolta [an avenue in the shopping district]. All along the waterfront there the Japanese had these little pillboxes that they had been in and used to shoot out of. But by this time the Filipinos had killed these Japanese, and they were lifting the dead bodies as we went by out of these pillboxes, or whatever they were, and pulling out their gold teeth. The Japs had a lot of gold teeth, you know."

Dead bodies of enemies and defenders lay sprawled on the streets, and the air was filled with nauseating odors. The Filipinos suffered horribly as the Japanese took revenge on them for their support of the Allies. In the course of the conflict tens of thousands of Filipino scouts fought a guerrilla war in the islands and served as an underground spy system. In Manila hundreds of innocent citizens were victimized, their houses looted and burned, people burned alive, raped, and tortured. Nola could remember a 4-week-old baby brought into the hospital with his little shoulder ripped and bleeding where a Japanese soldier had whirled him around on the point of a bayonet.

Much of Manila was damaged beyond repair. In the downtown area the fighting had shattered most of the buildings. In the rest of the city large portions were burned to the ground when shifting winds fed fires ignited in the initial onslaught. Public transportation was totally lacking. The water and sewage systems were partially destroyed, and electric power was nonexistent. Many of the bridges were gone, and most of the streets needed repaving.

MacArthur had not wanted to see this friendly city torn apart. He put a ban on using air attacks against Japanese positions in the city and placed curbs on the use of artillery. When the American forces came up against the power of the Japanese defenses, however, they had to fight fire with fire.

An estimated one hundred thousand Filipinos lost their lives compared with a total of 1,010 Americans killed in the fighting, and another 5,565 wounded. The Japanese lost sixteen thousand men in the struggle in and around the city

The general found his 7-room penthouse apartment on the top of the Manila Hotel almost totally demolished, including his valuable military library, his souvenirs, and two huge ceremonial vases that the Japanese emperor had given his father in 1905. On a visit to the city on February 27th he attended a ceremony at the Malacanan Palace to mark the reestablishment of the Commonwealth government. President Osmena and several cabinet members addressed the group, and when it was MacArthur's turn, he was so deeply moved he could not finish the speech he had prepared.

He transferred his headquarters to Manila just before the arrival of Jean, Arthur, and Ah Cheu, the amah, on March 6th. Jean MacArthur immediately threw herself into volunteer relief work, visiting former prisoners, paying hospital calls, and writing letters to families in the United States whose loved ones had been interned.

About this time, as Nola recounted, "We moved the medical headquarters from Leyte. We had all our records and everything in Manila. We went into a little office in the university there, not Santo Tomas but Philippine University. The Japanese still had part of the city [near] where the Manila Hotel is. That was where a battle was fought almost hand to hand, room to room.

"We were all given places to live. They gave me this house in Quezon City, which is near Santo Tomas [north of the Pasig]. Somebody by the name of Gonzales had lived in it before the Japs had taken it over. It was a lovely, big, three-bedroom house, but what the Japs had done was disable all the toilets. They were just shelled out. So we had a big Chick Sale out in the back, way at the backyard, and it was filled with rats.

"One night we were sitting, or standing, in the living room — I don't know if we were sitting because we didn't have much furniture — and Polly, who was my assistant, said, 'Oh, it can't be. It must be a cat. It can't be!' It was a rat that was about this big, and at night you'd be scared.

"The house had a dining room, a beautiful, big dining room with a lovely dining table and chairs. Then we noticed there was this trap door, and we opened up the trapdoor and went down, and here had been a Japanese spy station. There were some antipersonnel bombs — I asked somebody what they were — and other things down there. I got a couple of books that evidently they'd been using.

"I had a maid; they gave me a maid, too. Only it turned out to be two maids, and I said, 'Well, now, how is this?' The maid brought her companion, but we didn't use our kitchen at all. Some of the engineers had a house down the street, and they fed us most of the time. Otherwise we would go up to the mess. But the engineers had a cook, and they usually would say, 'Why don't you come down for dinner tonight?' You see, I was getting sicker and sicker."

Nonetheless, as director of nurses Nola continued on her inspection rounds. She guessed her illness "probably happened before I left Leyte ... but I kept going and kept going. After I went to Manila, I had hospitals up in Luzon that I had to go to. The Japanese still had a lot of territory. We were still fighting a war, you see. As always, I was the only woman in a plane at night. Sometimes I'd get on a plane that was filled with ammunition and sit on top of the ammunition and go up."

Medical units had poured into Luzon from the start of the invasion. In this campaign the openness of the terrain supported the orderly sequence of the chain of evacuation to a far greater extent than in jungle fighting. Medical staff still used portable hospitals near the fighting, but they were backed up by clearing and collecting companies with jeeps and ambulances to speed the wounded to field and evacuation hospitals near beaches and airstrips. Patients loaded onto airevac planes or surgically equipped LSTs for transportation to station and general hospitals in the rear.

The first station hospital arrived in Manila in late February in the midst of the fighting while crowds were celebrating in the streets as neighboring parts of the city burned. The 49th General Hospital arrived on March 1st, as the city was turning into a base. Other hospitals were quickly established north and west of the city.

A few weeks after the invasion began, the Sixth Army requested that nurses be sent to the Lingayen area on the first available hospital ship. By the end of January, Maj. Willa Hook, who had escaped from Corregidor in April 1942, came to the gulf as the chief nurse for Luzon. Within the next two weeks she found a way to get to Manila bringing gifts to her liberated friends in Santo Tomas with whom she had served in makeshift jungle hospitals.

In February staff members from several hospitals in Leyte came on a hospital ship, which discharged some of them at Subic Bay, northeast of Bataan, and others up the coast at Lingayen Gulf. More nurses came later from New Guinea. One of these was 2nd Lt. Agnes Troxell Paist, who remembered her fear of Japanese air attacks during a 5-day voyage from Hollandia past Southern Philippine islands still occupied by the enemy.

As the fighting continued on Luzon and elsewhere, the doctors were challenged by the number and complexity of medical problems. The Army's official campaign history would later reckon total battle casualties at forty-seven thousand for all the fighting on Luzon and the Southern Philippines, of which 10,380 were deaths and the rest wounded.

*Nonbattle* casualties for the Sixth Army on Luzon in the first half of 1945 alone were far greater — more than 93,400, most of them from infectious diseases. The history states, " … it is doubtful that any other campaign [of World War II] had a higher nonbattle casualty rate among American forces." The humid climate at sea level sapped the energies of soldiers who were exhausted from fighting in one campaign after another with no relief. In mountain areas hot, dry days and cold, wet nights lowered resistance to infection. The men also encountered new diseases against which they had no built-in defenses.

Nola was one of the nonbattle casualties, although at first she didn't recognize her illness. "By the time I got to Manila," she said, "I was having a lot of neuritis and losing weight, which I didn't mind. The doctors in the office all noticed it, but I didn't realize anybody did. What they were doing, I discovered later, was one of them would say to me — in the office we had surgical consultants and medical — 'I'm going up to such-and-such a hospital this morning. Have you any reason you want to go there?' And I'd say, 'Yes, I have.' We had them all around Manila.

"So we'd come back maybe around one o'clock, and he'd say, 'I think I might as well drop you off at your house. There's no need for you to come back to the office this afternoon.' And I'd say, 'I think maybe I need a rest.' They kind of took turns doing that, and I didn't catch on until later what was happening."

On April 23rd, USASOS headquarters issued a file note recommending that orders be issued placing Lt. Col. Nola Forrest on temporary duty at Base K, headquarters 8th Army in Leyte, and stating that "The Surgeon, 8th Army, has informally requested that [she] visit all hospitals now under 8th Army control."

Of course, Nola was in no condition to visit any hospital except as a patient. "I felt awful the last month or six weeks," she recalled. "They finally put me in the Johns Hopkins hospital out there [the 118th]. Then they said I had to be evacuated. They said I had to have complete bed rest. Eventually this leg got paralyzed, and this arm was paralyzed, the left arm. I had about six diagnoses. They thought it was polio at first. I was almost unable to feed myself. I was in pain most of the time."

Back in Manila the city was coming to life. By mid-March the lights were on. Part of the municipal water supply was functioning, and the port and harbor areas were put in workable condition by the Army engineers. Epidemics were averted by the speedy work of General Headquarters health, education, and welfare officers, although the VD (venereal disease) rate among American troops, again in contact with women, began to rise alarmingly.

Fighting persisted against Yamashita's forces south of Baguio and east of the city's boundaries even as the U.S. armed forces were occupying, rebuilding, bringing in supplies, and sending some people home. MacArthur assigned noncombat troops to clear debris in the devastated capital, to distribute relief, and to help reopen schools.

With order established, people were looking for entertainment. Nola had to miss a concert in which a singer introduced the "Pants" song written in her honor by Irving Berlin after their New Guinea dinner party. It went like this:

Oh, for a dress again
To caress again—in a dress again.
Covered up from your head to your toe,
We must hide what we'd like to show.
Oh, for a skirt again—just to flirt again,
There's no romance when you dance
Cheek to cheek and pants to pants.
Oh, for an old-fashioned dress!

On May 3, 1945, Nola Forrest received orders to proceed from Base K via air, ground or water transportation "for purpose of carrying out instructions," a standard phrase. That same day General Denit wrote a memorandum for her 201 (service record) file that summarized her role.

Part of his statement declared: "The superior manner in which you have executed the duties of this difficult office has been of inestimable assistance to me as Chief Surgeon. Particularly worthy of approbation was your assistance in the establishment of the policy ... whereby nurses are brought into newly occupied territory during the early stages of a campaign instead of remaining behind in staging areas ... The favorable effect of this policy on the morale of combat troops has now been recognized beyond question. Your own fearless presence with these nurses during the initial days of both the Leyte campaign and the battle for Manila was in keeping with the highest traditions of the service and set an example to be followed by the members of the Army Nurse Corps throughout the rest of this war."

The next week Nola sailed on the SS *Monterey* with Pauline Kirby, recently promoted to lieutenant colonel, who was returning to the States on rotation. The outside world was in ferment. President Roosevelt had died in April, a trusted leader gone from the scene, and the new president, Harry S Truman, was coping with a barrage of uncertainties. During the voyage, the war in Europe came to an end, and as peace emerged thousands of miles away, the nurses played bridge across Nola's hospital bed with an Army psychiatrist, who teased them about their ids and made them laugh.

On dismissing Nola, the 118th General Hospital in Leyte gave her diagnosis as "arthritis, nonsupperative, infectious, chronic, cervical, thoracic and lumbar spine, shoulder joints, and proximal phalangeal joints, 3 fingers, both hands." She was shipped to Letterman General Hospital in San Francisco, but within two days she was moved again, at General Kirk's behest, to Walter Reed Army Medical Center in Washington, D.C.

She remembered flying east in an airevac plane on which she was the only woman patient. The berths were stacked three deep with wounded men. When they stopped for refueling and stayed overnight, every patient was taken out on a litter and then put back in the plane the next morning.

The doctors at Walter Reed were baffled by Nola's condition. Her body hurt all over, and she could scarcely move or speak. After ruling out polio, the doctors tested her for amyotrophic lateral sclerosis, but her symptoms didn't quite match those for that disease. The Army surgeons observed her for five weeks, then shipped her back to California for observation and treatment at Torney General Hospital in Palm Springs. There Nola was glad to find that the principal chief nurse was Major Edna Traeger, her assistant in the Desert Training Center. The hospital even offered her some social life by trundling her out in her wheel chair for parties with the interns.

While the war continued, Nola received joyful news of two of her friends in Leyte. A mimeographed announcement of the marriage of Capt. Claire Whalen to Maj. Alan Enzor on 17 June 1945 turned up in her papers. Her bridge companions on the *John Alden* had taken their vows in the 118th General Hospital chapel.

According to the tongue-in-cheek announcement, "The bride wore a stiffly starched suntan shirt and Quartermaster-styled slacks with matching accessories: a suntan stitched fatigue hat, white hand-knitted sox and brown oxfords. [She] carried a bouquet of native gardenias," which she threw to the attending khaki-clad "lassies [who] broke two arms in the scramble."

On July 4th, MacArthur declared the Philippines liberated even as fighting went on in northern Luzon and the central and southern islands. Allied preparations were building for the invasion of Japan, and soon thereafter a wave of more than one thousand U.S. planes battered Tokyo for the third time, creating rings of fire that destroyed large parts of the city. British warships joined Americans in bombarding the coast.

The Japanese leaders were warned of a new, more powerful

weapon, which they ignored, and on August 6th, the first atom bomb in warfare was dropped on Hiroshima with one hundred and forty thousand killed. After a second one destroyed much of Nagasaki and most of its inhabitants, the Japanese emperor capitulated. The Americans celebrated V-J Day on August 15th in the midst of overwhelming relief at having averted slaughter on the beaches and the deaths of hundreds of thousands of young men from their own and Allied countries.

As the war thundered through its terrifying finale and the start of reconstruction, Nola Forrest tried to recover her health. In November she was sent briefly to Dewitt General Hospital in Auburn, California, and then back to Letterman where she stayed until June 1946. "I had porphyrial neuritis," she explained. "It was a captain at Letterman who had had a degree in biochemistry before he took up medicine [who] discovered the porphyrins [abnormal chemical compounds] in the blood. They didn't think of that at first.

"Since then the doctors have told me that they think it was due to DDT. You see, DDT was just in its inception, and they'd open up these bombs in the tents up in New Guinea, and the whole tent would be so thick you could almost cut it with a knife. But you needed it for mosquitoes. They thought it was probably some chemical in my system that reacted unfavorably with that. There was nothing to do for it. It just wore itself out."

By the summer of 1946, Nola was up and about. Her mobility was coming back, but the Army doctors told her she would never be able to perform active duty again. "I'd had [almost] twenty-two years by then," she reflected, "and I wasn't ready in my mind to stop. But physically I knew I couldn't do it."

On September 30, 1946, the Army announced the retirement of Lt. Col. Nola Forrest from active service "on account of disabilities incident thereto." The order was signed by Dwight D. Eisenhower, Army Chief of Staff.

In the Army medical files a hand-written justification was found for Nola's retirement on 70 percent disability. It gives her record of service and the nature of her illness. The record also includes an early performance evaluation signed by Gen. Guy B. Denit, which states, "Secure, loyal, efficient officer. Inspires confidence by her tact, leadership, judgment and common sense."

Looking back on the sweep of events Nola commented, "You felt you were a part of history. I used to say at the time, 'The next time there's a war, I'd like to come back as a second lieutenant instead of lieutenant colonel, the boss.' They seemed to have a lot more fun ... No, I think I enjoyed all the experiences, and I enjoyed seeing how wonderfully our men conducted themselves as patients and as soldiers and how everyone seemed to work together."

In testimony to the part she played, Nola Forrest was awarded the Bronze Star Medal and Army Commendation Ribbon, the American Campaign Medal, the American Defense Service Medal, the Asiatic-Pacific Campaign Medal with 2 bronze service stars (Philippine Islands and New Guinea Campaigns), and the Philippine Liberation Ribbon.

# Chapter 10

# Epilogue

"**B**y the time they were retiring me, I was much better," Nola could say. In the fall of 1946, no longer undergoing treatment, she was sharing an apartment in Portland, Oregon, with her old friend Phoebe Nelson Karolchnik. The next year she moved to California where, spurred by her restless nature and the postwar housing shortage, she lived in temporary quarters, first in Pasadena and then in San Francisco, sometimes with friends.

On a tour of the Southwest she described "a very terrible automobile accident. I went over a 20-foot embankment, sixty-five miles an hour, had fourteen fractures. I was broken in pieces, but that isn't all. It was a frosty morning down in Texas. There'd been a norther about, and nobody found us for a while.

"A rancher's wife heard us — I kept kind of poking on the horn — and she sent her sons and her husband out, and they picked me up and stuffed me into the back seat of a 2-door Ford, and we drove to a doctor's office, which was about twelve miles. The doctor said, 'Oh,' he said, 'I just quit. I've got to get you to a hospital.'

"My ankle was way out, but a lot of these fractures were ribs and collar bone and all that sort of thing. So I had them call Brooke [Army Medical Center], which was two hundred miles away at San Antonio. I knew the chief nurse very well. I asked them if they had an ambulance, and they said yes. Well, it turned out to be a hearse. They took me those two hundred miles. I was there for seven months. I had a long rest."

Once her bones had knit, Nola still limped badly from her misaligned ankle. An Army surgeon she knew at Letterman persuaded her to come there and let him operate. He spent months and months resetting the ankle until it finally was straightened so that she could walk in a normal manner.

During most of the 1950s Nola made her home in San Francisco, a city she loved. She helped to found a book and gift shop at Grace Episcopal Church and managed the volunteers. She taught home nursing for the Red Cross as a volunteer herself. She took a trip on a freighter to the Orient.

But in the midst of her new activities she faced another setback. In 1953, while staying in Portland, she was diagnosed with cancer of the uterus and right away called her friends in Letterman for a second opinion. The doctors arranged a bed for her, examined her, and operated on the spot. She recovered completely and never had a recurrence.

By now the urge to wander had returned in earnest. "I started to travel," Nola recounted. "I've been to every continent and around the world a couple of times. That's what I love. I'm no good at cooking and keeping house."

In 1960 she spent ten weeks covering western Europe in a series of one-night hops from Brussels to Luxembourg to Italy — Rome, Venice, Florence, Padua, Assisi, Sorrento, Capri — then on to Nice, Avignon, Lucerne, and Paris. From there she took in Copenhagen and three days later departed for Scotland — Glasgow, Edinburgh, Loch Lomond, and Stirling — looking up Forrest cousins in a weeklong whirl. Circling back, she went to Windermere, Stratford, Oxford, and London, then to New York and Washington and dropped in on her parents in Minneapolis on her way home.

In 1961, Nola Forrest was ordered back to active duty in the Historical Division of the surgeon general's office in Washington, D.C., to work for three months on the history of Army nurses in the Southwest Pacific Area in World War II. This unpublished history, produced with Eileen Brady, her former assistant, proved an invaluable background source for supplementing Nola's personal memories of the war.

Perhaps this assignment reminded her of the stimulation of wartime days in the nation's capital. Whatever the reason, she moved in 1962 into the Army Distaff Hall, a retirement center in Washington for Army women. Here she made her home for the next ten years, except that she was often away for months at a time.

In 1965 her diaries show that she spent two months in Los Angeles then went up to San Francisco to see the Sequoias, then to Carmel, and back to Washington. The next year she traveled to Spain and Morocco.

In 1968 she cruised on the *Monterey* to Bora Bora, Moorea, Tahiti, and Rarotonga. This was the same ship that had taken her home from the Philippines, now back in service as a luxury liner. She sailed on to New Zealand where she was welcomed to Auckland by three Scottish second cousins once removed. To introduce these ladies we must take another look at Nola's ancestors. In so doing, the reader may discern some genetic causes for Nola's chosen profession and her love of travel.

Nola's grandfather, Dr. James Forrest, was the eldest of three brothers. About the time Dr. Forrest emigrated from Scotland to the United States, the youngest brother, William ("Will") Forrest, a mariner, had decided to settle down in New Zealand after several voyages, each of several months. The third brother, Andrew ("Andy") Forrest, had moved to New Zealand a few years earlier, sailing from Britain with his bride only a few weeks after he married. None of the three brothers ever returned to Scotland.

The brothers were the sons of Dr. William Hutton Forrest, Nola's great grandfather. After obtaining his degree in medicine from the University of Edinburgh, the young doctor found no opening for practice in his native town of Stirling. So in 1819 he set out for Cuba to start his career in medicine. On the way to Cuba, his ship stopped at Charleston, South Carolina. Not finding Cuba to his liking, he returned to Charleston and started his practice in a rural district inland.

After a few years he contracted yellow fever. About the same time, a practice opened up in Stirling when his father's cousin, Dr. John Forrest, died. Dr. William Hutton Forrest returned to Scotland, and a family story says he was accompanied by his black servant Toby, who helped to nurse him back to health. Toby stayed in Scotland, the story goes, and is buried with his employer in the family's cemetery plot.

This explains why on Nola's cruise on the *Monterey*, she was welcomed in Auckland, New Zealand, by Will's eldest daughter Isabel, then in her nineties, along with her younger sisters, Margaret and Moubray. Later they all dined on board the ship as it lay at anchor in the Bay of Islands.

The *Monterey* cruise combined Nola's love of travel with another lifelong passion — serious bridge playing. After leaving New Zealand, her ship sailed to Sydney where she had become a member of a team of sixteen Americans competing with Australian champions. On the opposite side of the world she cruised to Bermuda five or six times playing in bridge competitions. She sharpened her game from casual playing in prewar years to the expert level, a point or two short of grand master rating.

Her travels continued. In 1970 she flew from Washington to Seattle and there boarded a freighter, the *Hong Kong Mail*, for Yokohoma, Kobe, and Osaka, the site of Expo 70. She went on to Kyoto, Inchon, and Seoul, then to Okinawa, Taiwan, Hong Kong, and Singapore, where she left by the freighter *Philippine Mail* for Madras.

The next year Nola couldn't wait to dash off again. With her long-time friend and fellow Army nurse Elsie Schneider, she traveled around the world. They started in San Francisco and went to Honolulu, Tokyo, Hong Kong, Bangkok, Katmandu, New Delhi, Agra, and Jaipur, where Nola rode on an elephant. The two friends continued to Bombay, Nairobi, Mombasa, Addis Ababa, Cairo, Athens, and London, returning to New York and home to Washington, D.C.

Nola's forays into foreign lands may have made the Army Distaff Hall seem tame because she left its protective atmosphere in 1972 and stayed away for ten years. First, she went to live in Monterey, California, but by 1975 she was residing in Clearwater, Florida, near her younger sister Marjorie. Four years later she was back in Portland, Oregon. Not until November 1981 did Nola return to her former Washington residence.

Opened in 1961 to provide a home and care for Army widows and other family members and retired female Army officers, the Army Distaff Hall was renamed Knollwood in 1989 and began to accept men, couples, and career officers from all the armed services. Nola never again left its sheltering environment on a permanent basis, although she left a record of a coach trip in 1985 to England, Wales, and Scotland.

As she grew older, her pace slowed down, and she would shake her head and say, "I just can't do that any more." She continued to keep in touch with many people, played bridge as long as possible, and felt sad as her old companions died, one after the other.

In July 1995, Nola's career was celebrated when she was featured in a *Washington Post* series on World War II in which men and women recalled events that marked their service. The next year, on her 96th birthday, she was visited by Brig. Gen. Anna Mae Hays, the first woman in the history of the U.S. military to attain general officer rank, in 1970, as chief of the Army Nurse Corps. General Hays brought Lt. Gen. Ronald R. Blanck, surgeon general of the Army, to hear Nola tell about Norman T. Kirk, wartime Army surgeon general, and her memories of the war.

During World War II, ninety-six American lives were saved for every one hundred men wounded, a remarkable record. Postoperative care was a major factor. Although preceded by frontline surgery, effective medication, and rapid evacuation from combat zones, the lives of fighting men were ultimately saved by vigilant nursing. The nurses worked with each other and the rest of the medical team to keep patients alive when first admitted and to deliver care throughout the stages of recovery.

In August 1945 when the Japanese surrendered, more than fifty-six thousand ANC members were on active duty. During the war 215 had died in service, sixteen from enemy action. More than two-fifths of the active registered nurses in the United States had volunteered for military service, and by its end some 27 percent of all active professional nurses were serving with the armed forces. By September 1946, when Nola was retired, only eighty-five hundred Army nurses remained in the Corps.

Peace continued to bring swift and significant change. On April 16, 1947, Congress enacted PL 36 establishing the Army Nurse Corps in the Regular Army and providing permanent commissioned officer status for its members. Army nursing was now recognized as a profession. In 1951 a directive relieved nurses of all custodial and housekeeping duties. At the same time innovations in training and responsibility developed during World War II and later in the Korean War were becoming permanent features of the service.

New opportunities opened up allowing nurses to specialize in fields like psychiatric nursing, operating room techniques, pediatric nursing, and anesthesiology. Nurses who were interested could also earn masters degrees in health care administration, and many of them took on management roles. In 1955 male nurses were permitted to join the Corps reserves and a decade later given full Army commissions.

In 1957, Congress enacted another important law affecting Army nurses. PL 155 provided for five colonels and 105 lieutenant colonels in the Corps plus other upgrades in status and pay. Mandatory retirement at age sixty was retained. Nola Forrest was then fifty-seven years old. She had been retired too soon to receive the promotion that probably would have been given her had her health permitted, and the chance for even greater career achievement and retirement pay.

Yet Nola remarked on more than one occasion that she would not like to be a member of the modern Army Nurse Corps. Even without the special bonds that arose from the war experience, "Once we all were single, we all lived together, and we had a wonderful camaraderie," she said. "When you came on a new post, you could always find someone you knew. Today you have less contact with the patients. You drive to work, do your job, and drive away. It's not the same."

She had always warmed to people, certainly those in her professional life, with whom she sustained long-time friendships, but also those whom she met on her endless travels. She seemed to see her life as a series of passages from one scene to another, with herself at the ready for a new experience or a new friend. Among Nola's papers her nephew found this handwritten poem:

I have always loved journeys, long or short,
But the journey on which I shall
Some day embark—Is it long or short?
No one seems able to tell me.
Through the windy night something is coming up the path
Towards the house.
I have always hated to wait for things,
I think I will go to meet whatever it is.

On July 30, 1999, Nola Forrest went to meet the unknown presence that was coming toward her. She had foreseen the end for many months as her voice became weaker and her movements feebler. She still showed a spark of warm recognition whenever I came to visit her and could still pull from her memory illuminating bits of information. She managed to reach her 99th birthday in June, but every response in those last few months was an effort. She was very, very tired.

Eleven days after her death, a memorial service was held in the Old Post Chapel at Fort Myers in Arlington, Virginia, and the ashes of Lt. Col. Nola Forrest were placed in a grave on the nurses' hill in Arlington National Cemetery. As fate determined, her assigned plot adjoined that of her dear friend, Lt. Col. Elsie Schneider.

On a knoll overlooking the hill stands a marble statue of a lady that embodies the "tenderness, compassion, competence, courage and humanity of military nurses," in the words of a nurse historian. In 1928, Ida Hube, who would later sustain her imprisoned friends in Manila, conceived the idea of a memorial monument and contributed the first one hundred dollars.

In 1938 the statue, designed by Frances Luther Rich, was dedicated by Julia Stimson, who stated that the sculptress had it carved in "immortal marble a symbol of the spirit of nursing." She added, "... We present this guardian of our comrades in their eternal sleep, and as an inspiration to all who devote their lives to the service of others."

Nola Forrest, now among them, was given full military honors, which included a band and horse-drawn caisson that led the procession from the chapel to the gravesite. There she received a salute of three volleys from a 7-man rifle squad, the flag was presented to her nephew, Dr. Robert Forrest, and a bugler played taps. It was a beautiful day.

Nola Forrest, age 95, at Knollwood, Washington, DC, July 26, 1995
(photo by Nancy Andrews *Washington Post*)

# SOURCE NOTES

Nola Forrest's two recorded oral history interviews and twenty-five off tape interviews along with her papers — orders, appointments, letters, memorandums, diary notes, and news clippings — make up the chief primary sources for this book. Interviews with other people make up the rest. Many additional sources have been used to fill out the broader background and also to check Nola's recollections against existing documents. A full bibliography of all the sources is appended. These notes give references to sources listed in the bibliography.

**PREFACE**

"Heroic Nurses Get Thanks of Nation," *The New York Times*, 25 February 1945.

Difficulties of the Pacific war are discussed in *The Pacific War Revisited*, eds., Gunter Bishof and Robert L. DuPont, "Introduction," by D. Clayton James, pp. 10 and 34.

Policies in different World War II theaters whereby Army nurses were brought into or near combat areas were noted in Mary Ellen Condon-Rall and Albert E. Cowdrey, *Medical Service in the War Against Japan*, p. 269. For change in policy in the Leyte invasion see oral history of Nola Forrest, July 31, 1987 and off tape interviews, September 27, 1994 and September 11, 1998.

The history of the start of the Army Nurse Corps and relative rank is given in Mary T. Sarnecky, *A History of the U.S. Army Nurse Corps*, pp. 42- 51, 56, 57, and 142-148; for number of nurses in WWI, see p. 122.

The summaries of Nola Forrest's career are based on her oral histories, July 8, 1987 and July 31, 1987 as well as on her papers.

Quote on skills of Colonel Blanchfield, see Nola Forrest oral history, July 8, 1987. Quote on duties of chief nurses in World War II, see Pauline Maxwell, "History of the Army Nurse Corps, 1776-1948," chapter VII, p. 46. Twenty-six lieutenant colonels in 1944, see records of the Army Nurse Corps.

Law granting nurses relative rank with equal pay as male officers, see Sarnecky, pp. 266 and 267.

The quote on Nola's preference for face-to-face meetings is found in the report by Eileen Brady and Nola Forrest, "The Pacific Theater in World War II," "The Philippines,"p. 4. Her participation in the Desert Training Center field trials see off tape interview, November 21, 1998.

Marie Adams quote is from her letter, March 5, 1945, in Nola's papers. Statement that Nola "took after" no one is from off tape interview, November 3, 1997. Competitiveness at the bridge table is from author interview with Dr. Robert Forrest, July 26, 1996. Nola's romance, engagement, and letters from friends are in her papers. Statement that she didn't want to talk about a fiancé is from off tape interview, October 7, 1996.

Description of the closeness between members of the Army Nurse Corps, see off tape interview, August 8, 1997. See also Barbara Tomblin, *G.I.Nightingales*, p. 188.

Quotes by General Denit, see letter to Nola, May 3, 1945, in Nola's papers.

Discussion of Nola's experience of fear or lack of fear, see off tape interviews November 3, 1997; March 7, 1998, and September 11, 1998.

Number of nurses in World War II, see Maxwell, chapter VIII, p. 2. Lives saved, P.A. Kalisch and B. J. Kalisch, *The Advance of American Nursing*, p. 349. Nola's quote, "Could all that have happened…" is from off tape interview, June 16, 1998.

## CHAPTER 1. THE START OF THE JOURNEY

Nola's story of her early life until joining the Army Nurse Corps is chiefly based on her first oral history interview of July 8, 1987, supplemented by off tape interviews. References to family are found in off tape interviews, November 29, 1988; January 30, 1996; April 10, 1996, and October 7, 1996 as well as author interview with Dr. Robert Forrest, July 26, 1996.

The descriptions of Lake Wilson, Minnesota, are taken from *Lake Wilson, 1882-1982*, ed., Gary Richter; the quote, "When the first settlers came …" is on page 1. Background on homesteading was also provided by "A

Brief History of Land Settlement in Minnesota" from the Department of the Interior, Bureau of Land Management, Minnesota Pre-1908 Homestead & Cash Entry Patents, CD-ROM.

Nola's education, nurses training, early employment, and entrance into ANC reserve are in off tape interviews January 13, 1997; March 26, 1997; October 1, 1997, and November 3, 1997. Reference to De Witt Wallace is from *Who's Who in America, 1996-1969*, Vol. 35.

Women who volunteered for service in World War I, see *Into the Breach: American Women Overseas in World War I*, by Dorothy and Carl J. Schneider.

The bio on Julia Stimson is based on Patricia Spain Ward in *Dictionary of American Biography, 1946-1950*, p. 788.

Recruitment of college women for nurses training in World War I, see P. A. Kalisch and B. J. Kalisch, *The Advance of American Nursing*, pp. 197 and 221; also on treatment of student nurses in earlier years, pp. 201, 202, 206-208, and 220.

Background on veterans hospitals, from Geoffrey Perrett, *America in the Twenties*, pp. 132-133.

The description of American railroads in the 1920s is based on *Rails Across America*, ed. Will Steeds.

Change to "relative rank," see Sarnecky, pp. 142-148; Army Nurse Corps pay scales, p. 139.

Nola's acceptance in ANC reserve, her appointment in the regular Corps, and her orders to Manila are found in her papers, as are references to her romance. Dora Thompson's career is noted in Sarnecky, pp. 100 and 136-138.

## CHAPTER 2. OVERSEAS DUTY

America in 1928 is described in Geoffrey Perrett, *America in the Twenties*, pp. 321-327, 361-363, 337-340, 315, 316, and 373.

Nola's description of life in Manila is chiefly found in her oral history of July 8, 1987, supplemented by off tape interviews.

Background on Manila and the governing of the Philippines was drawn from entries on Manila, on Leonard Wood, and on Henry L. Stimson in *The New Columbia Encyclopedia*, 1975 edition, and from Emily Hahn, *The Islands: America's Imperial Adventure in the Philippines*, pp. 164-170. Atmosphere and social life are depicted in the Ralph Graves novel, *Share of Honor*.

Julia Stimson's career was covered in Mary T. Sarnecky, "Julia Catherine Stimson: Nurse and Feminist," in *IMAGE*, 25 (Summer 1993), pp. 113 and 119. The description of Manila is drawn from Robert Ross Smith, *The War in the Pacific*, pp. 237-240.

Social life and living arrangement are in off tape interviews, May 4, 1996; March 26, 1997, and November 3, 1997, as well as in Nola's letters home. The routine in Sternberg General Hospital is mentioned in off tape interview, May 4, 1996, supplemented by Denny Williams, *To the Angels*, p. 24, and Elizabeth M. Norman, *We Band of Angels*, pp. 3 and 4. Nola's acquaintance with Martha Jane Clement and Norman T. Kirk is mentioned in off tape interview, May 29, 1996.

Illness of Phoebe and Nola's own travels are covered in off tape interviews, April 10, 1996; May 29, 1996; March 26, 1997, and May 3, 1997. Description of the trip to Japan and China is in Nola's letters home. The reference to "Japs" with comment on wartime hatred is covered in David M. Kennedy, *The American People in World War II*, Part II, pp. 385-387. Leave policy for Army nurses, Julia Flikke, *Nurses in Action*, p. 80.

The trip to the Southern Philippines is covered in off tape interviews, March 26, 1997; May 3, 1997, and November 3, 1997 .

The gathering depression is described in Perrett, *America in the Twenties*, pp.373-375, 377-379, and 383. Nola's request for "continuation of service" is found in her papers.

Quiet years in military circles, see Geoffrey Perret, *Old Soldiers Never Die*, p. 152 and Richard M. Ketchum, *The Borrowed Years, 1938-1941*, pp. 126-128.

Nola's change of station is in her papers. Her description of her Walter Reed assignment and her transfer to Fitzsimons are in her off tape interview, May 29, 1996. Tea with Julia Stimson is in off tape interview, September 11, 1998. Phoebe's recovery and marriage are in off tape interviews, April 10, 1996; March 16, 1997; May 3, 1997; May 29, 1997; November 3, 1997, and September 11, 1998.

The death of Nola's brother Robert is mentioned in off tape interviews, October 7, 1996 and March 26, 1997 and also in a letter from Dr. Robert Forrest, March 12, 1999.

Nola's change of station to Schofield Barracks is shown in her papers. Number of Army nurses on active duty in the 1930s is covered in Maxwell, chapter VI, p. 34. Nola's descriptions of her life on Hawaii are in off tape interviews, April 10, l996; May 4, 1996; November 3, 1997, and January 24, 1998.

Descriptions of Schofield Barracks and its history were taken from *Encyclopedia of Historic Forts*, and Brian Nichols, "Schofield Barracks," in *Honolulu* magazine, November 1981.

Nola's assignment to Fort Lewis as well as the letters of condolence from her friends on Mac's death are in her papers.

## CHAPTER 3. MOBILIZATION

The descriptions of Fort Lewis in the late 1930s and during 1940 and 1941 are taken from Joe D. Huddleston, "Fort Lewis, A History," and "History of Fort Lewis," from HRC 331. Posts-Lewis, Ft., Washington. References to Gen. George C. Marshall are from Leonard Mosley, *Marshall: Hero for Our Times*.

Nola's account of life at Ft. Lewis is from oral history interview, July 8, 1987, supplemented by off tape interviews. For her travels to Canada and travels in the fall of 1939, see off tape interviews, May 3, 1997 and January 24, 1998. Leaves of absence are shown in her papers.

Descriptions of the World's Fairs are found in "Fairs and Expositions" in *The Encyclopedia Americana International Edition*, Vol. 10 and David Gelernter, *1939: The Lost World of the Fair*, pp. 16, 17, 24, 25, 37, and 400.

Dwight D. Eisenhower's account of his part in troop training at Fort Lewis and elsewhere is from his *Crusade in Europe*, pp. 4-10. For Eisenhower's role at the war's begining, I drew on Merle Miller, *Ike the Soldier*, pp. 305-311.

Nola's duty at the Presidio in Monterey, California, see off tape interviews, January 30, 1996; April 10, 1996, and May 4, 1996.

Call-up of the National Guard is in Maxwell, chapter VII, pp. 1 and 2. German onslaught, fall of France, declaration of Italy, see Kennedy, pp. 14 and 15.

Changes in public opinion, see Allan Nevins, "How We Felt About the War," pp. 4-6 in *While You Were Gone*, Jack Goodman, ed., and Ketchum, pp. 468 and 469. Reference to the Roper poll is from Gelernter, p. 27.

Nola's promotion to first lieutenant is in her papers. Memories of Mamie and John Eisenhower noted in off tape interviews, January 30, 1996 and April 10, 1996.

For national mood at Christmas in 1940, see William K. Klingaman, *1941: Our Lives in a World on the Edge*, pp. 30 and 31. Prosperity from war orders, see Kennedy, p. 39.

Nola's transfer to Walter Reed General Hospital in 1941 is in her papers. Nurses over forty sought for administrative positions, see Flikke, p. 74. Nola's reassignment to the Nursing Division is in off tape interview, January 21, 1995. The staff of four in the division is noted in Maxwell, chapter VII, p. 7.

Nola's quotes on start of the war are in oral history, July 8, 1987 and off tape interview, January 30, 1996.

Demand for and recruitment of nurses are taken from several sources: Maxwell, chapter VII, pp. 4, 28, and 29; Sarnecky, pp. 171-179 and 269; Bonnie Bullough and Vern L. Bullough, *The Emergence of Modern*

*Nursing*, p.188; and interviews conducted by Col. Katherine Jump and Maj. Constance Ferebee with Col. Florence A. Blanchfield in March and April 1968.

Army strength, including medical, is in Maxwell, chapter VII, p. 4. Nurses in demand, see Sarnecky, p. 177 and Maxwell, chapter VII, p. 29.

History of reserve hospitals is in Sarnecky, pp. 80 and 81. Nola's description of reserve hospitals is in oral history, July 8, 1987 and off tape interviews, January 21, 1995 and May 29, 1996. Information on organization of reserve hospitals is in Clarence McKittrick Smith, *United States Army in World War II: The Technical Services: The Medical Department*, pp. 141 and 143.

Nola's quote on promotions is in oral history, July 8, 1987. Move of nursing headquarters is in Maxwell, chapter VII, p.8. Uniforms are discussed in Sarnecky, pp.273-275.

The Army War Show is mentioned in Maxwell, chapter VIII, p. 38; in Nola's oral history and off tape interviews, May 29, 1996 and May 3, 1997; an article by Rex White in the *Detroit Free Press*, n.d.; and Dorothy Sutherland, "Army War Show," in *R-N*, October 1942. Requirements for Army nurses are given in an untitled article by Nola Forrest in an Army Medical Bulletin of 16 February, 1942 and in Maxwell, chapter VII, pp. 42 ff.

Representative Bolton's legislative actions to aid American nursing are in Kalisch and Kalisch, pp. 272, 273, 340, and 341; and in Bullough and Bullough, p. 191.

Descriptions of the train wreck are in the July 8, 1987 oral history; in "20 Die in Blazing Wreck of 3 B. & O. Trains in Pass," *The New York Times*, 25 September, 1942; "Riders Calm, Say Wreck Witnesses," *The Washington Post*, 25 September, 1942; and "Rail Crash Death Toll Set at 14," *The Washington Post*, 26 September, 1942.

## CHAPTER 4. TRIAL RUN

Pay Readjustment Act of 1942, see Sarnecky, p. 268.

Nola's descriptions of the Desert Training Center are in oral history, July 8, 1987, supplemented by off tape interviews. The development of the Center is described in Sidney L. Meller, "The Desert Training Center," "Prefatory Note", and pp. 1-5, 13, 19, 39, 52-55, and 76. The quote on the climate and account of Patton's training methods are in Martin Blumenson, *The Patton Papers, 1940-1945*, pp. 58, 59, and 75.

Nola's assignment, promotion to major, and mission statement are in her papers. Base pay for that rank is in Flikke, p. 81. Norman Kirk pinning oak leaves on Nola's shoulders is in off tape interview, May 29, 1996.

Nola's April 8, 1943 report to Blanchfield is in her papers.

Description of conditions of military training, see Mellor, p. 60. Nola's quote on the heat is in her oral history, July 8, 1987. Her reports to the commanding general, Com Zone and to the surgeon general's office are in her papers.

Nola's description of her living quarters is in off tape interview, January 24, 1998.

The quote from the letter of the chief nurse at the 32nd Evacuation Hospital in Yuma is in Nola's papers.

The story of the pregnant nurse is in off tape interviews, January 21, 1995 and January 30, 1996. Colonel Blanchfield's ruling on "cyesis" is in Edith Aynes, *Nightingale to Eagle*, p. 209.

Nurses taking infiltration course reported in the *Slayton Herald*, July 1943, and *The New York Times*, October 9, 1943. The nurse rescuing patients from a fire was reported in the *Los Angeles Times*, July 10, 1943, and also in *The American Journal of Nursing*, 43, p. 774. The nurse rescuing a soldier from drowning is in Nola's report to Hq Com Z, August 9, 1943, and also in *The American Journal of Nursing*, 43, p. 859.

Recreation in small towns and in the training center is covered in Mellor, pp. 26-30. Nola's time off and conversation with Nelson Eddy is in off tape interview, January 24, 1998. Her 10-day leave is shown in her papers.

Movement of the 13th General Hospital from Spadra to New Guinea is cited in Smith, *The Medical Department*, p. 157; C-AMA closing down, Mellor, p. 88.

Nola's orders to report to Washington, her report to the C-AMA surgeon, and her January 1, 1944 report to Colonel Blanchfield, as well as letter from Blanchfield, October 13, 1943 and letter from Ida Danielson, October 5, 1943 are in her papers.

## CHAPTER 5. DOWN UNDER

Ida Danielson quote is in her letter, March 19, 1943, in Nola's papers.

Quote on "beehive of activity" and description of nursing headquarters is taken from Flikke, p. 69. Danielson's transfer to London is cited in Carolyn M. Feller and Deborah R. Cox, *Highlights in the History of the Army Nurse Corps*, p. 19.

Publicity and movies about military nurses, see Kalisch and Kalisch, pp. 343 and 344. The nurses' embarrassment over *So Proudly We Hail*, see Norman, pp. 125-129.

Army nurses killed at Anzio cited in *Highlights*, p. 16. Nola's promotion to lieutenant colonel shown in her papers. Twenty-six Army nurses at that rank, in records of the Army Nurse Corps Historian. Her quotes on decision to send her to SWPA are in her oral history, July 8, 1987. The description of Martha Jane Clement is taken from Frazier Hunt, " 'Ma' Clement and her Guinea Girls," *Cosmopolitan* magazine, September 1944, pp. 54, 55, 145, and 146.

Full temporary commissions for Army nurses is noted in *Highlights*, p.16.

Nola's assignment, clothing authorizations, and departure dates are in her papers. Article from *Chicago Tribune* is dated July 26, 1944. Account of Nola's voyage and arrival in Australia is in oral history, July 8, 1987. Description of Brisbane is from *The New Columbia Encyclopedia*, 1975 ed.

Nola's official duty date, travel authorizations, and directives are in her papers.

End of New Guinea campaign, see Thomas J. Cutler, *The Battle of Leyte Gulf*, pp. 8, 9, and 14.

Australia huge supply base, William Breuer, *Retaking the Philippines*, p. xviii. Hospitals moving north, Condon-Rall/Cowdrey, p. 145. Denit's statement to Nola, in off tape interview, September 11, 1988. Nola's description of life in Lennon's Hotel, in oral history, July 8, 1987.

The account of MacArthur's assignment to Australia and his early days there is based on several sources: Perret, *Old Soldiers Never Die*, pp. 282-287; Breuer, pp. xiii, xiv, and xviii; Douglas MacArthur, *Reminiscences*, pp. 140-145, and William Manchester, *American Caesar*, pp. 250-269.

The account of the Japanese attack on Darwin, see Martin Gilbert, *The Second World War*, p. 302. The Japanese military position and the challenge facing MacArthur are based largely on Cutler, pp. 7-9. The Battle of the Coral Sea is based on Gilbert, p. 322 and Kennedy, pp. 106 and 107. The account of the Papuan campaign is from Perret, *Old Soldiers Never Die*, pp. 294-297, 304-306, 315, 324, and 325, and on Charles R. Anderson, *Papua*, CMH Pub 72-7.

Evacuation of the wounded and role of portable hospitals is described in Condon-Rall/Cowdrey, pp. 72, 73, 78, 79, 141-144 and 206, 207, 214, and 215; stresses of disease and climate, pp. 140 and 145-147.

Arrival of the first fixed hospitals in Port Moresby, including nursing conditions in 10th Evacuation Hospital and 171st Station Hospital, are based on Condon-Rall/Cowdrey, pp. 144-145. Conditions in 153rd Station Hospital described in *The American Journal of Nursing*, 44, p. 676. Visit of Captain Clement to Port Moresby is in Frazier Hunt *Cosmopolitan* article.

Malaria and other diseases are discussed in Condon-Rall/Cowdrey, 137-141; in MacArthur, pp 155 and 156, and in Eileen Brady/ Nola Forrest, "The Pacific Theater in World War II: New Guinea," p. 2.

Tension between nurses and enlisted male medical workers noted in Condon-Rall/Cowdrey, pp. 269-270.

Arrival of first nurses in Australia is in Brady/Forrest, "Australia," pp. 1 and 2; also in Maxine Russell, *Jungle Angel*, pp. 44 and 45. The award to

Fellmeth is listed in "Awards and Decorations to Nurses," a typed report in the archives of the Army Nurse Historian.

Mary Connell's account of the voyage to Australia and subsequent moves is found in Mary T. Sarnecky's oral history of Connell, September 13, 1994, pp. 6-9, and 11. The escape of the nurses from Corregidor is in Perret, *Old Soldiers Never Die*, p. 289; in Flikke, pp. 185-187, and in Brady/Forrest, "Australia," p. 4. The choice of Willa Hook and Catherine Acorn to stay on is cited in Norman, p. 115. The voyage by submarine is in Lucy Jopling, *Warrior in White*, pp. 47-55. Hortense McKay's choice to stay and her duties in Sydney and concern with uniforms are in Russell, pp. 45-47.

Arrival and disposition of nurses and hospitals in Australia, and 4th General Hospital the biggest and best equipped are mentioned in Brady/Forrest, "Australia," pp. 14 and 15.; also the total of twenty-three hospitals in Australia by the end of 1942.

Erma Myers's account of her time in Australia is taken from her diary and letters.

New bases in New Guinea and assignment of nurses mentioned in Brady/Forrest report, "New Guinea," pp. 3-5. Connell at Base B, see her oral history.

Fitting out of two hospital ships is described in Brady/Forrest, "Australia," pp. 14 and 15. Bases moving north are mentioned in Condon-Rall/Cowdrey, pp. 204, 205, and 254. Hortense McKay's move is in Russell, pp. 48 and 49. Nola's orders to Hollandia are in her papers.

## CHAPTER 6. VOYAGE TO LEYTE

Nola Forrest quote is from her second oral history, July 31, 1987. Hollandia as "an anthill of activity," Tomblin, p. 54. Description of changes in hospitals in Hollandia, Maxwell, chapter XIV, p. 109.

Cost of the Papuan campaign for the Allies, from Geoffrey Perrett, *There's a War to be Won*, p. 239. The advance of the New Guinea campaign, Perrett, pp. 258-266; Edward J. Drea, *New Guinea*, CMH publication 72-9, and MacArthur, pp. 191-195. Suffering of the soldiers on Aitape, Albert E. Cowdrey, *Fighting for Life*, p. 193; American casualty total on Biak, pp. 194-195. Awards to Biak medics, Condon-Rall/Cowdrey, p. 214.

The arrival of hospitals on Biak and the description of daylight there are cited in Brady/Forrest report, "New Guinea," p. 12. Nola's quote about the fighting on Biak is from oral history, July 8, 1987.

Cost of fighting on Aitape and awards for heroism, Drea. p. 28.

Chain of evacuation, Condon-Rall/Cowdrey, pp. 78, 79, 214 and 215; penicillin in theater, p. 205; spread of use, Cowdrey, p. 187. The chain of evacuation on New Guinea, Cowdrey, p. 185.

Erma Meyers' accounts of duty at the 360th Station Hospital on Goodenough Island are found in her papers.

Nola's descriptions of living conditions and food in Hollandia are in oral history, July 31, 1987. The women's confinement to the WAC compound, see Brady/ Forrest report, "New Guinea," p. 11; description of nurses' clothing, pp. 2 and 10; reference to beauty parlors, p. 7. The male officer's quote is in Mattie E. Treadwell, *The Women's Army Corps*, p. 426.

The description of the building of MacArthur's house in Hollandia is in William Manchester, p. 348; the location of MacArthur in Brisbane is from D. Clayton James, *The Years of MacArthur*, Vol. II, Appendix B, pp. 800-801.

Nola's account of the phone call from Brickey is from oral history, July 8, 1987 and off tape interview, October 7, 1996. The background on the assemblage of the invasion armada is from Cutler, pp. 41-43 and 54-59; quote on the "time table" is on p. 55.

Nola's conversations with Denit and his assistant (Colonel Dart) are in oral histories, July 8, 1987 and July 31, 1987 and off tape interview, July 13, 1988. Nola thought that Denit probably did not know of the decision to send nurses in with the invasion. According to Condon-Rall/Cowdrey, "the chief surgeon's voice was heard dimly" with the task forces ... [he] sometimes got a chance to review and comment," p. 253; yet "Departing from earlier SWPA policy, General Denit allowed female nurses into Leyte on the twenty-ninth," p. 323. To what extent, if any, was this Denit's decision? Nola's statement that Colonel Hagins had requested her was made in off tape interview, March 7, 1998.

The account of the ride of Nola Forrest and Eileen Brady to the *John Alden* and their boarding is taken from oral histories, July 8, 1987 and July 31, 1987 and from off tape interviews, June 27, 1996 and July 31, 1996. The description of Liberty ships is from Thomas Allen and Norman Polmar, eds., *America at War, 1941-1945*, p. 503.

The legs of the *John Alden* from Finschhafen to Aitape to Hollandia are found in "War Diary" of Commander Service Force, Seventh Fleet, for September and October 1944, showing ship arrivals at and departures from Hollandia; in the "Report of Voyage, SS John Alden" by Robert Roger McAdams, USNR, Commanding Officer, Naval Armed Guard, February 4, 1945, and in the "Quarterly Historical Report" by Lt. Col. Harry Wolowitz of the Headquarters, 2nd Field Hospital to the Chief Surgeon, RESOS, 5 January 1945; all these in the Office of Naval Records, National Archives and Records Administration (NARA).

Nola's account of her voyage to Leyte is from oral history, July 8, 1987 and from off tape interviews, January 22, 1995; July 13, 1996; June 28, 1997, and September 11, 1998. The references to Catherine Acorn as chief nurse of the 2nd Field Hospital and the nurses' assignnment to the 36th

Evacuation Hospital are in Maxwell, chapter XIV, p. 20.

The account of the Battle of Leyte Gulf is from Cutler, pp. 198-205, 221-222, 257-264, 268, 269, and 285; also from Kenndy, p. 403; and James. Vol. II, p. 564.

The arrival of the nurses in Tacloban harbor and their experience caring for casualties under fire in the Palo cathedral are described in oral history, July 8, 1987; in an article in *The American Journal of Nursing*, 45, p. 44, and in the letter to Col. Florence Blanchfield, quoted in Maxwell, chapter XIV, p. 21. Another account is contained in a SWPA press release, "Nurses Work in Oldest Cathedral in the Philippines," n.d.

The account of early military operations in Leyte is from Samuel Eliot Morison, *History of United States Naval Operations in World War II*, Vol. XII, p. 155.

The quote on performance of the field nurses is from Nola Forrest's letter to Colonel Blanchfield, in her papers, n.d. Bronze Star awards are noted in Maxwell, chapter XIV, p. 32. Nola's request to General Crabbe is from her oral history, July 8, 1987. Her travel permission is in her papers.

## CHAPTER 7. NINE WEEKS IN NEW GUINEA

The account of Nola's trip to Hollandia from Leyte is found in her oral history, July 8, 1987. Her travel orders are in her papers. Heirarchy of nurses and visiting duties are in Maxwell, chapter XIV, p. 9.

Nola's comments on Pauline Kirby as her assistant and descriptions of travel by plane are in her oral history, July 31, 1987. The mention of cribbage is in off tape interview, January 13, 1997, and the comment on lack of fear from off tape interview, September 11, 1998.

The description of New Guinea is from oral history, July 31, 1987, and the account of nurses sent into islands in the north is from oral history, July 8, 1987. The story about Pauline Kirby is in off tape interview, June 28, 1997.

The movement of hospitals to Leyte is noted in Condon-Rall/Cowdrey, p. 320 and also in Maxwell, chapter XIV, p. 23. The reception of patients in the 54th General Hospital in Hollandia and the description of the first day is from Kenneth B. Coldwater, "The Professional View," in "54th in Review," n.p., n.d., quoted in Maxwell, chapter XIV, pp. 112 and 113. The description of building the 54th General Hospital is in Condon-Rall/Cowdrey, p. 258.

The record of the hospital ships is found in Maxwell, chapter XIV, pp. 23-26. The description of hospital ships is in Condon-Rall/Cowdrey, pp. 258-259; the reference to Geneva Convention of 1929 is in footnote in Condon/Rall-Cowdrey, p.363. The statement on hospitals reaching planned capacity is from the Brady/Forrest report, "New Guinea," p. 8.

The description of Christmas at the hospital is from Coldwater, as quoted in Maxwell chapter XIV, pp. 113-115.

Nola's description of the environment is in Brady/Forrest, "New Guinea," pp. 1 and 2 and the health of the nurses on p. 8. Other references to nurses' health are in the Brady/Forrest report, "The Philippines," p. 7; in Jopling, pp. 87 and 88, and in Maxwell, chapter XIV, pp. 320-323. The description of the New Guinea barracks is from Myrtle E. Arndt, "The Women's Angle," in "54th in Review," quoted in Maxwell, chapter XIV, p. 320. References to health, morale, and evacuation are in Maxwell, chapter XIV, pp. 318 and 321.

Erma Myers' health problems and wedding are described in her papers (letters home).

Nola's description of soldiers in the hospitals and her travels in New Guinea are from her oral history, July 31, 1987. Her description of her visit to the 268th Station Hospital is in her off tape interviews, January 25, 1995 and June 27, 1996. The history of that hospital and other hospitals with African American personnel is taken from Tomblin, pp. 123, 163, 177, 178, and 193. The number of Negro nurses serving at war's end is cited in Clarence Smith, p. 111.

Nola's account of dining with the missionaries and meeting Irving Berlin is in off tape interviews, July 13, 1996 and March 7, 1998. Description of the sing-sing is from Mary Virginia Fox, *Papua New Guinea*, pp. 7, 40 and 41. Her comment on Berlin is in Marylou Tournignant interview in *The Washington Post*, July 26, 1995. Nola's account of dinner with the Navy is in oral history, July 31, 1987.

The account of the invasion of Leyte and MacArthur's arrival onshore is taken from MacArthur, pp. 215-218. The establishment of his headquarters is described in Manchester, p. 390 and in James, Vol. II, p. 583. Descriptions of the fighting on Leyte are taken from Rafael Steinberg, *Return to the Philippines* (Time-Life Books), chapter 3 and from Brueur, pp. 79, 81, and 82. The incident of disease is cited in Judith Bellefaire, *The Army Nurse Corps*, p. 26. Contaminated soil is noted in Brady/Forrest, "The Philippines," p. 3.

The opening of Base K and the conditions there are described in Maxwell, chapter XIV, p. 108. Most of the beds in Leyte not ready and equipment in short supply cited in Condon-Rall/Cowdrey, pp. 325 and 326. Twenty-six nurses in Palo the only women on the island for a month is noted in Maxwell, chapter XIV, p. 29.

Morale of flight nurses on Biak is noted in Maxwell, chapter XIV, pp. 27 and 28; their training and conditions of work are described in Jopling, pp. 71-73. The arrival of WACs in Leyte is cited in Treadwell, pp. 428 and 429. The arrival in Leyte of the land-based nurses is cited in Maxwell, chapter XIV, pp. 31 and 33.

Nola's description of her dinner on the Dutch hospital ship is in her off tape interview, June 28, 1997. The end of the Leyte campaign is described in Perrett, *There's a War to Be Won*, p. 507. Nola's description of Christmas on Leyte is in her oral history, July 31, 1987. Her account of Christmas Day with Eichelberger and his staff is in off tape interviews, July 13, 1996 and November 18, 1996.

The arrival of the 133rd General Hospital and other hospital units and nurses is noted in Maxwell, chapter XIV, pp. 30 and 31. Hortense McKay's arrival at the 133rd is described in Russell, p. 52. Hospitals moving "up the line"is cited in Maxwell, chapter XIV, pp. 104, 106, and 107. McKay's move to the 126th General Hospital and her descriptions of the work and her quote are from Russell, pp. 52 and 53. Twenty thousand casualties moved to Leyte in the first two motnhs of 1945 is cited in Bellafaire, p. 28.

Nola's official move to Leyte is noted in Maxwell, chapter XIV, pp. 4 and 6. The quote about landing safely is in a letter from Mary Menek to Colonel Blanchfield, January 28, 1945 in the Army Nurse Corps Historian archives. Nola's quotes on Casey and her staff are from her oral history, July 8, 1987. Her activities in Leyte are based on a report to headquarters, January 1945, in the Army Nurse Corps Historian archives.

## CHAPTER 8. FULL CIRCLE

The plan for drafting nurses is referred to in Maxwell, chapter, XIV, p. 10. Data on ANC staff levels in January 1945 are in Brady/Forrest, "The Philippines," p. 2; also in Maxwell, chapter XIV, p. 10.

Plans for the invasion of Luzon are drawn from MacArthur, p. 239 and Perret, *Old Soldiers Never Die*, pp. 437 and 438. The action on Mindoro is taken from Dale Andrade, *Luzon* (CMB Pub 72-28), pp. 6 and 67, and Gilbert, pp. 617 and 618.

The description of the invasion is drawn from Brueur, pp. 109-114. The description of the fleet's advance is based on James, Vol. II, pp. 619 and 620, and MacArthur, p. 242. The advance of the U.S. infantry toward Manila is taken from Perret, *Old Soldiers Never Die*, pp. 438 and 443-446; James, Vol. II, p. 633, and Robert Smith, p. 221.

MacArthur's quote on starving prisoners is from *Reminiscences*, p. 246. The rescue at Cabanatuan is fully covered in Hampton Sides, *Ghost Soldiers*, pp. 258-290. The description of the 1st Cavalry advance to Santo Tomas is drawn from the above sources and from Robin Prising, *Manila, Goodbye*, pp. 177 and 178.

The description of the use of Santo Tomas University as an internment camp is based on Frederic Stevens, *Santo Tomas Internment Camp*, pp. 6 and 7; Hahn, pp. 214-216, and A.V.H. Hartendorp, *The Santo Tomas*

*Story*, pp. xiii and 7-12. The next eleven paragraphs describing the early experiences of the internees, the way they organized themselves and were controlled by their captors drew on Stevens, pp. 80-85, 369, and 485; Hartendorp, pp. 7, 8, 10-16, 20-29, 32-36, 43, 45, and 53, and Marie Adams' testimony, "In the matter of the killing, mistreatment, etc.," p. 6.

The arrival of 55 Army nurses from Corregidor and their experiences on Bataan and Corregidor are cited in Bellafaire, pp. 5 and 6; Norman, pp. 76-87, 104-109, 130, 135-141; Jopling, pp. 44 and 45; Alice Clarke, *The American Journal of Nursing*, 45, p. 343; Ullom, pp. 3-5, and Denny Williams, *To the Angels*, pp. 86, 87, and 115-119.

The nurses' first few weeks in Santo Tomas are described in Norman, pp. 151-156 and in Josephine M. Nesbit, "History of the Army Nurse Corps in the Philippine Islands," pp. 37, 38, 40, and 41. The organization of the camp hospital is found in Condon-Rall/Cowdrey, p. 376.

Denny Williams's descriptions of life in the camp are from her book, pp. 127, 138-140, 146, and 171.

Activities of medical teams are cited in Hartendorp, p. 21; Adams, pp. 5 and 6, and in Nesbit, p. 41.

The arrival of ten Army nurses who had failed to escape is described in Norman, p. 157. Constant interest in food is cited in Hartendorp, p. 38. The first Christmas is described in Williams, pp. 145, 159, and 160.

The treatment of the escapees from Santo Tomas is detailed in Hartendorp, pp. 39-43. That event and the treatment of the prisoners in Fort Santiago are also described in Adams, pp. 2-5. A detailed account of his own treatment in the fort was given in Stevens, pp. 326-345.

The move of almost 800 internees to Los Banos is described in Williams, pp. 174 and 175, and James, Vol. II, p. 643. Medical help from the Red Cross and relief supplies via the *Gripsholm* in 1943 are cited in Condon-Rall/Cowdrey, p. 376; Adams, pp. 4 and 5, and Ella Grimmestead, *The American Journal of Nursing*, 44, pp. 31 and 32. Christmas under another commandant is described in Williams, p. 184; see also Stevens, pp. 369 and 427.

Military police takeover of the camp and worsening of conditions taken from Stevens, pp. 369 and 429-431. Williams quote on hunger is from her book, p. 185. Defensive measures by the Japanese and increasing inmate sickness are described in Stevens, pp. 434-437, and 442-444; Hartendorp, p. 268; Adams, p. 6, and Norman, pp. 184-187. Lines from minstrel show are in Williams, p. 188; end of camp entertainment is noted in Hartendorp, pp. 280 and 281.

Confiscation of money, searches, and punishments are cited in Stevens, pp. 446, 447, 449, 463, and 468; in Nesbit, p. 41, and Prising, p. 172. Raids by American planes in the fall, further restrictions, and arrest of camp leaders are taken from Stevens, pp. 454-473 (inmate log). The last two or three months of starvation and death are cited in Adams, pp. 7 and 8; physical depletion of people noted in Stevens (log), pp. 471 and 472; Condon-Rall/Cowdrey, p. 338, and Hartendorp, p. 364. Conditions in last month and fear of massacre are noted in Stevens (log), p. 475, and Hartendorp, p. 370.

The rescue scene is based on Stevens, p. 482 and Williams, pp. 200-202. Negotiations with the Japanese were recorded in Steinberg, pp. 124-130. Supply operations of American soldiers were described in Prising, pp. 185-190. The description of MacArthur's visit to Bilibid and Santo Tomas is based on Robert Smith, p. 254; James, Vol. II, p. 639, and Roger Egeberg, *The General*, pp. 134-136, and 139.

Nursing conditions in Base K are described in Brady/Forrest, "The Philippines," pp. 5 and 6. Orders to Nola Forrest to fly to Santo Tomas with rescue medical team are in her papers, a news clip (unidentified), and off tape interviews, January 21, 1995 and November 18, 1996. Her descriptions of the flight and the arrival at Santo Tomas are in her oral history, July 31, 1987.

The Japanese attack on the camp, the emergency medical setup, the arrival of the 893rd Medical Clearing Company, and the arrival of Nola's group are from Adams, p. 9; Williams, p. 219; Norman, p. 210; Maxwell, chapter XIV, pp. 50 and 53, and Brady/Forrest, "The Philippines," p. 8. Nola's quote on the 67 nurses is from her oral history, July 31, 1987. The inclusion of the last two nurses is noted in Nesbit, p. 42.

Nola's description of her reunion with friends is from off tape interview, September 11, 1998. Further quotes on her meeting with friends are from her oral history, July 31, 1987. The notation of internee loss of weight is from Peter C. Richards, ed., "Liberation Bulletin," February 3, 1945.

Nola's description of the nurses' treatment and the Japanese shelling is from her oral history, July 31, 1987. Her medical group giving care under fire is noted in Maxwell, chapter XIV, p. 54. The quote by the rescued nurses is from Clarke, p. 345. The Bronze Star citation is in Maxwell, chapter XIV, p. 59, and the departure of the 893rd clearing company is noted in Maxwell, chapter XIV, p. 58.

Nola's description of the exodus of the interned nurses is from her oral history, July 31, 1987. Her memory of the couple getting married is from off tape interview, June 28, 1997. The description of the wedding is from Norman, p. 210, as well as the fact that Josie Nesbit married a man from the camp, p. 250. The list of other nurses who married men they knew in Santo Tomas is in Ullom, p. 242. Williams's description of their departure from the camp is in her book, pp. 220 and 221.

Nola's description of their trip to Leyte, awards, and departure for home
are from her oral history, July 31, 1987. Capt. Chadbourne's trip to
Hollandia for uniforms is cited in Maxwell, chapter XIV, p. 56.1. The
nurses' description of their welcome in Leyte is from Clarke, p. 345 and
also from Russell, pp. 54 and 55. Their meal on the plane is from a menu
in Nola's papers. The statement about Capt. Davison is from Maxwell,
chapter XIV, p. 57. The news account of the nurses' arrival in San
Francisco is from *The New York Times*, February 25, 1945. Nola's added
information on the nurses is from her oral history, July 31, 1987.

The story about Norman Kirk's annoyance at being kept out of the combat
area is from Nola's off tape interviews, May 29, 1996 and July 31, 1996;
see also James, Vol. II, p. 890.

The story of the Los Banos rescue is from Robert Smith, p. 427; Maxwell,
chapter XIV, p. 59, and Condon-Rall/Cowdrey, p. 338. The description of
the Santo Tomas internees is from Prising, pp. 203-205. The account of
their disposition is from Stevens (log), p. 483.

## CHAPTER 9. REENTRY

The weekly report by Nola, dated February 25, 1945, is in the Army Nurse
Corps Historian archives.

Nola's 10- to 12-hour days and soreness of left arm noted in handwritten
review of 16 April 1964 of Nola's record in Official Army Records
(Nola's papers). The move of the medical group to Manila is mentioned
in Nola's oral history, July 31, 1987; also in Maxwell, chapter XIV, p. 4.

The description of the battle of Manila is taken from Robert Smith, pp.
240-246, 249, and 271; from James, Vol. II, pp. 41-45, 640-642, 644, and
647, and from Steinberg, pp. 120 and 136. Nola's description of her tour
of the city is from her oral history, July 31, 1987. The statistics on the loss
of life on both sides are from Robert Smith, p. 307.

The description of MacArthur's return to Manila is from James, Vol. II, pp.
41-45, 646-648, and 654, and from Brueur, pp. 253-255. Nola's description of her house and her visits to hospitals is from her oral history, July
31, 1987.

Nola refers to using a "Chic Sale." This was an outhouse that derived its
name from a comic act and book by Charles ("Chic") Sale, who invent-
ed a rural carpenter named Lem Putt, whose specialty was building fancy
outhouses. In time, the actor's name, to his dismay, became the slang
name for an outhouse. To quote his wife, "In his wildest dreams, Charlie,
who died in 1936, would not have believed that American soldiers, in our
war against Japan, would be quartered on lonely Pacific islands where
their only laughable encounter would be stumbling on an enclosure bear-
ing a homemade 'Chic Sale' sign," from an article by Marie Sale, "Charles

'Chic Sale' And His Boomerang," Specialist Publishing Company, Burlingame, CA, n.d.

Medical chain of evacuation and arrival of hospitals in Luzon is described in Condon-Rall/Cowdrey, pp. 336 and 339. The arrival of Army nurses in Luzon is noted in Maxwell, chapter XIV, pp. 37 and 3 9. Major Hook's reunion with nurses in Santo Tomas is noted in Maxwell, chapter XIV, p. 53. Memories of voyage to Luzon of Agnes Troxell Paist are in her interview, dated August 6, 2003.

Statistics on casualties in the Philippines campaign are taken from Robert Smith, pp. 652 and 653. Nola's description of her illness is in her oral history, July 31, 1987. The file note recommending temporary duty at Base K is in her papers. The description of Manila rebuilding is from James, Vol. II, pp. 41-45, and 653 and 654. "Pants" song in letter from Berlin, December 1, 1947, in Nola's papers; see also *Washington Post*, 26 July, 1995.

The orders for Nola to proceed from Base K are among Nola's papers, as is the letter of May 3, 1945 from Denit. Her return to the States with Major Kirby on rotation is cited in Maxwell, chapter XIV, p. 3.

The 118th hospital diagnosis is in Nola's papers. Nola's memories of her flight east and later treatments are found in off tape interviews, January 21, 1995, January 22, 1995, and January 13, 1997, and in her oral history, July 31, 1987. The moves to different hospitals are shown in her papers, as is the account of the Whalen-Enzor wedding.

The account of the ending of the war is from Kennedy, pp. 420-422, 424 and 425.

Nola's statements on her diagnosis, the end of her career, and her reflections on her war experience are found in oral history, July 31, 1987. The announcement of her retirement is found in her papers. Denit's earlier performance evaluation is quoted in a handwritten AGO review in Official Army Records, "Forrest, Nola Gladys N701473," dated 16 April 64. The list of Nola's decorations is in her papers.

## CHAPTER 10. EPILOGUE

Nola's quote is from her oral history, July 31, 1987. Her early postwar moves are shown in her papers and the Robert Forrest chronology. The description of the automobile accident and subsequent treatment is from her oral history, July 31, 1987 and from off tape interview, January 21, 1995.

Nola's activities in San Francisco are from the Robert Forrest chronology and from off tape interview, January 13, 1997. The description of the cancer incident is from off tape interviews, January 21, 1995 and January 13, 1997. Nola's quote on love of travel is from her oral history, July 31, 1987. Quote on "no good at cooking" is from author conversation with Robert Forrest, July 26, 1996.

The accounts of Nola's 1960 travels and her work in 1961 on the SWPA nurses' history are found in her papers and in the Robert Forrest chronology, as are her move to the Army Distaff Hall and mention of further travels. Her visit to her cousins in New Zealand is described in off tape interview, April 10, 1996. The family history is an account by Robert Forrest, and it is also covered in off tape interviews, January 30, 1996; October 7, 1996, and August 1, 1997, as well as author interview with Robert Forrest, July 16, 1996.

Nola's bridge playing is mentioned in off tape interviews, April 10, 1996 and June 28, 1997 and in the Robert Forrest interview, July 16, 1996. Her travels in 1970 and 1971 and her move away from the Army Distaff Hall and later return are shown in the Robert Forrest chronology, which is based on her travel diaries and other papers. The description of the Army retirement center is from *Bugle Call*, Winter 1997.

Nola's appearance in the news is found in *The Washington Post* article by Marylou Tousignant, July 26, 1995, HA Section, p. 7. The account of the visit of the Army surgeon general on her 96th birthday is in off tape interview, July 27, 1997. Anna Mae Hays attaining general officer rank is noted in *Highlights*, p. 43.

Saving of American lives in World War II and the proportion of nurses who served are noted in Kalisch and Kalisch, pp. 348 and 349. The number of nurses on active duty at war's end is given in Sarnecky, p. 278. The number of ANC deaths in World War II is given in Department of the Army, "Army Battle Casualties and Nonbattle Deaths," p. 112. The number of active registered nurses volunteering and the percent serving are cited in *The American Journal of Nursing*, 45, p. 683. The number of Army nurses on active duty in September 1946 is noted in *Highlights*, as is the law authorizing permanent commissions for Army nurses, p. 19.

The description of measures toward greater professionalization of Army nursing is from Sarnecky, pp. 395 and 397- 398.

Nola's quote on not wanting to be a member of the Army Nurse Corps today is from off tape interviews, March 26, 1997; May 3, 1997, and August 1, 1997. Her poem is in her papers. The notice of her death was published in *The Washington Post*, August 5, 1999. Background on military interments at Arlington National Cemetery is given in the article by Tom Warren, "Hallowed Ground," *The Washingtonian*, June 1999, pp. 52 - 57.

The history of the military nurse memorial in Arlington National Cemetery is from Sarnecky, pp. 165-166. Gun salute and presentation of flag, see "Military Funerals" in *The Officer's Guide: A Ready Reference on Customs*, etc., pp. 218-223.

# BIBLIOGRAPHY

## Primary Sources

### MANUSCRIPTS AND PERSONAL PAPERS

Aarons, Erma Myers. Papers (in Army Nurse Corps Historian archives).

Adams, Marie, Field Director, American Red Cross. Testimony "In the matter of the killing, mistreatment, abuse, lack of medical treatment and food rations of American internees at the Santo Tomas Internment Camp, Philippine Islands." Washington, D.C.: War Department, War Crimes Office, 11 June 1945.

Brady, Col. Eileen W., and Lt. Col. Nola G. Forrest. "The Pacific Theater in World War II." MS in files of U.S. Army Center of Military History, Office of Army Nurse Corps Historian. Washington, DC, n.d.

"Forrest, Nola Gladys N701473" two review-of-status handwritten papers from AGO files, dated 14 Mar 50 and 16 April 64.

Forrest, Nola. Papers (in possession of Dr. Robert B. Forrest, nephew).

Forrest, Nola. Brief paper prepared for the Army Medical Bulletin, no title (requirements for Army nurses), February 16, 1942.

Forrest, Robert B. "Nola Gladys Forrest — A Life" (chronology of Nola Forrest's career and travels plus copies of articles by and about her and her poem), n.d.; "Eulogy," August 10, l999.

Forrest, Robert B. Letter to Eleanor Stoddard, March 12, 1999.

"History of Fort Lewis." No author, n.d.

Huddleston, Joe D. "Fort Lewis: A History." Fort Lewis, WA: Office of Historian, 1986.

Manek, Mary. Letter to Colonel Blanchfield, January 28, 1945.

Maxwell, Lt. Col. Pauline."History of the Army Nurse Corps, 1775-1948." Washington, DC, 1976. MS in files of U.S. Army Center of Military History, n.d.

McAdams, Robert Roger, Lt. (jg), USNR, Commanding Officer, Naval Armed Guard. "Report of Voyage, SS John Alden," 4 February 1945.

Meller, Sgt. Sidney L. "The Desert Training Center and C-AMA." Study No. 15. Washington, DC: Army Ground Forces, 1946.

Nesbit, Josephine M., lst Lt. ANC. "History of the Army Nurse Corps in the Philippine Islands, September 1940 - February 1945." MS in files of the U.S. Army Center of Military History, Office of Army Nurse Corps Historian, n.d.

Richards, Peter C., ed. "The Liberation Bulletin of Philippine Internment Camp No. I." Manila, Philippines, February 3rd, 1945.

Ullom, Madeline M. "The Philippine Assignment: Some Aspects of the Army Nurse Corps in the Philippine Islands, 1940-1945." MS in the files of the U.5. Army Center of Military History, Office of Army Nurse Corps Historian, n.d.

Ullom, Madeline M. "Testimony Submitted on Behalf of the United States Army Nurses of the American Defenders of Bataan and Corregidor to Senator Dennis DeConcini, Member of the United States Veterans Affairs Committee, Phoenix, Arizona, by Lieutenant Colonel Madeline M. Ullom, United States Army Nurse Corps, Retired," 26 January 1982. MS in the files of the U.S. Army Center of Military History, Office of the Army Nurse Historian.

## INTERVIEWS

Blanchfield, Col. Florence A.: Oral history transcript of interviews by Col. Katherine Jump and Maj. Constance Ferebee, March and April 1963, at Army Center of Military History.

Campbell, Joan Malkenson: Oral history interview by Eleanor Stoddard, March 9, 1986 (transcript at California State University, Long Beach archives).

Connell, Mary B.: Oral history interview by Col. Mary Sarnecky, September 13, 1994 (transcript in Army Nurse Corps Historian office).

DeWan, Mary Jane: Oral history interview by Hermann J. Trojanowski, January 28, 1999 (transcript at University of North Carolina at Greensboro Oral History Collection).

Forrest, Nola: Oral history transcripts, July 8, 1987; July 31, 1987 (transcripts at California State University, Long Beach archives).

Forrest, Nola: Off tape interviews with author as follows:

November 29, 1988
September 29, 1993
September 27, 1994
January 21, 1995

January 22, 1995
January 30, 1996
April 10, 1996
May 4, 1996
May 29, 1996
June 27, 1996
July 13, 1996
October 7, 1996
November 18, 1996
January 13, 1997
March 26, 1997
May 3, 1997
June 28, 1997
August 1, 1997
October 1, 1997
November 3, 1997
January 24, 1998
March 7, 1998
June 16, 1998
July 13, 1998
September 11, 1998

Forrest, Robert: Author interview, July 26, 1996.

Hays, Brig. Gen. Anna Mae (Ret.): Author interview, August 11, 2003.

Moore, Maj. Constance J., Army Nurse Corps Historian: Author interview, January 20, 1996.

Paist, 1st Lt. Agnes Troxell (Ret.): Author interview, August 6 and 22, 2003.

Rosenbaum, Ruth: Oral history interview by Eleanor Stodddard, dated March 28, 1988 (transcript at California State University, Long Beach archives).

# Secondary Sources

## BOOKS

Aynes, Edith. *From Nightingale to Eagle: An Army Nurse's History.* Englewood Cliffs, New Jersey: Prentice-Hall, Inc., 1973.

Bischof, Gunter, and Robert L. DuPont, eds. *The Pacific War Revisited.* Baton Rouge and London: Louisiana State University Press, 1997.

Blumenson, Martin. *The Patton Papers: 1940-1945.* Boston: Houghton Mifflin Company, 1974.

Breuer, William B. *Retaking the Philippines: America's Return to Corregidor and Bataan: October 1944-March 1945.* New York: St. Martin's Press, 1986.

Bullough, Bonnie, and Vern L. Bullough. *The Emergence of Modern Nursing.* New York: The Macmillan Company, 1964.

Bullough, Vern L., and Bonnie Bullough. *History, Trends, and Politics of Nursing.* Norwalk, CT: Appleton-Century Crofts, 1984.

Condon-Rall, Mary Ellen, and Albert E. Cowdrey. *The Medical Department: Medical Service in the War Against Japan.* Washington D.C.: U.S. Army Center of Military History, 1998.

Connaughton, Richard M. et al. *The Battle for Manila.* Novato, CA: Presidio Press, 1995.

Cowdrey, Albert E. *Fighting for Life: American Military Medicine in World War II.* New York: The Free Press, A Division of Macmillan, 1994.

Cutler, Thomas J. *The Battle of Leyte Gulf, 23-26 October 1944.* New York: HarperCollins Publishers, 1994.

Egeberg, Roger Olaf. *The General: MacArthur and the Man He Called 'Doc.'* New York: Hippocrene Books, 1984.

Eisenhower, Dwight D. *Crusade in Europe.* New York: Doubleday, 1948.

Flikke, Col. Julia O. *Nurses in Action.* Philadelphia: J.B. Lippincott Company, 1943.

Fox, Mary Virginia. *Papua New Guinea.* Chicago: Childrens Press, Inc., 1994.

Gelernter, David. *The Lost World of the Fair.* New York: The Free Press, 1995.

Gilbert, Martin. *The Second World War: A Complete History.* New York: Henry Holt and Company, 1989.

Goodman, Jack. ed. *While You Were Gone: A Report on Wartime Life in the United States.* New York: Simon and Schuster, 1946.

Goodwin, Doris Kearns. *No Ordinary Time: Frank & Eleanor Roosevelt: The Home Front in World War II.* New York: Touchstone: Simon & Schuster, 1994.

Graves, Ralph. *Share of Honor.* New York: Henry Holt and Company, 1959.

Hahn, Emily. *The Islands: America's Imperial Adventure in the Philippines.* New York: Coward, McCann & Geoghegan, 1981.

Hartendorp, A.V.H. *The Santo Tomas Story.* New York: McGraw-Hill Book Company, 1964.

Hartmann, Susan M. *The Home Front and Beyond: American Women in the 1940s.* Boston: Twayne Publishers, 1982.

Holm, Maj. Gen. Jeanne M., USAF (Ret.). *Women in the Military: An Unfinished Revolution.* Novato, CA: Presidio Press, 1982.

James, D. Clayton. *The Years of MacArthur: 1880-1941.* Vol. I. Boston: Houghton Mifflin Company, 1970.

_____. *The Years of MacArthur: 1941-1945.* Vol. II. Boston: Houghton Mifflin Company, 1945.

Jeffrey, Jaclyn, and Glenace Edwall, eds. *Memory and History: Essays on*

*Recalling and Interpreting Experience*. Lanham, MD: University Press of America, Inc., 1994.

Jopling, Lucy Wilson. *Warrior in White*. San Antonio, TX: The Watercress Press, 1990.

Kalisch, P.A., and B.J. Kalisch. *The Advance of American Nursing*, 3rd. ed. Philadelphia: J.B. Lippincott Company, 1995.

Kaminski, Theresa. *Prisoners in Paradise: American Women in the Wartime South Pacific*. Lawrence, KS: University Press of Kansas, 2000.

Kennedy, David M. *The American People in World War II*, Part II. New York: Oxford University Press, 1999.

Kerr, E. Bartlett. *Surrender and Survival:The Experience of American POWs in the Pacific, 1941-1945*. New York: William Morrow and Company, Inc., 1985.

Ketchum, Richard M. *The Borrowed Years, 1938-1941: America on Her Way to War*. New York: Random House, 1989.

Klingaman, William K. 1941: *Our Lives in a World on the Edge*. New York: Harper & Row Publishers, 1988.

Litoff, Judy Barrett, and David C. Smith, eds. *We're in This War, Too: World War II Letters from American Women in Uniform*. New York: Oxford University Press, 1994.

MacArthur, Douglas. *Reminiscences*. New York: McGraw-Hill Book Company, 1964.

Manchester, William. *American Caesar*. Boston: Little, Brown and Company, 1978.

Miller, Merle. *Ike the Soldier: As They Knew Him*. New York: G.P. Putnam's Sons, 1987.

Morison, Samuel Eliot. *History of United States Naval Operations in World War II, Vol. XII: Leyte, June 1944-January 1945*. Boston: Little, Brown and Company, 1958.

Mosley, Leonard. *Marshall: Hero for Our Time*. New York: Hearst Books, 1982.

Mydans, Shelly Smith. *The Open City*. Garden City, New York: Doubleday, Doran and Company, 1945.

Nevins, Allan, and Henry Steele Commager. *A Short History of the United States*. New York: Modern Library, 1957.

Norman, Elizabeth M. *We Band of Angels: The Untold Story of American Nurses Trapped on Bataan by the Japanese*. New York: Random House, 1999.

Perret, Geoffrey. *Old Soldiers Never Die: The Life of Douglas MacArthur*. New York: Random House, 1996.

Perrett, Geoffrey. *America in the Twenties: A History*. New York: Simon and Schuster, 1982.

_____. *There's a War To Be Won: The United States Army in World War II*.

New York: Random House, 1991.

Prising, Robin. *Manila, Goodbye*. Boston: Houghton Mifflin Company, 1975.

Pullman, Sally Hitchcock. *Letters Home: Memoirs of One Army Nurse in the Southwest Pacific in World War II*. Granby, CT: The Quickprint Centers, 1997.

Richter, Gary, ed. *Lake Wilson, 1882-1982*. Lake Wilson, MN: Lake Wilson Centennial Book Committee, 1982.

Russell, Maxine Kaiser. *Jungle Angel: Bataan Remembered*. Brainerd, MN: Bang Printing Company, 1988.

Sale, Marie. *The Specialist*. Burlingame, CA: Specialist Publishing Company, n.d.

Sams, Margaret. *Forbidden Family: A Wartime Memoir of the Philippines, l941-1945*. Madison, WI: The Wisconsin University Press, 1989.

Sarnecky, Mary T., Colonel USA (Ret.). *A History of the U.S. Army Nurse Corps*. Philadelphia: University of Pennsylvania Press, 1999.

Schneider, Dorothy, and Carl J. Schneider. *Into the Breach: American Women Overseas in World War I*. New York: Viking, 1991.

Sears, Stephen W., ed. *Eyewitness to World War II: The Best of American Heritage*. Boston: Houghton Mifflin Company, 1991.

Sides, Hampton. *Ghost Soldiers: The Epic Account of World War II's Greatest Rescue Mission*. New York: Anchor Books, A Division of Random House, Inc., 2001.

Smith, Clarence McKittrick. *United States Army in World War II: The Technical Services: The Medical Department: Hospitalization and Evacuation, Zone of Interior*. Washington, D.C.: Department of the Army, 1956.

Smith, Robert Ross. *United States Army in World War II: The War in the Pacific: Triumph in the Philippines*. Washington, D.C.: Center of Military History, United States Army, 1984.

Stapleton, Darwin H., and Cathryne A. Welch, eds. *Critical Issues in American Nursing in the Twentieth Century: Perspectives and Case Studies*. Guilderland, NY: Foundation for the New York State Nurses Association Inc., 1994.

Steeds, Will, ed. *Rails Across America: A History of Railroads in North America*. New York: SMITHMARK Publishers Inc., 1993.

Steinberg, Rafael, and the editors of Time-Life Books. *Return to the Philppines*. Alexandria, VA: Time-Life Books, 1979.

Stevens, Frederic H. *Santo Tomas Internment Camp, 1942-1945*. Stratford House, Inc. (limited private edition), 1946.

Toland, John. *But Not in Shame: The Six Months After Pearl Harbor*. New York: Random House, 1961.

Tomblin, Barbara Brooks. *G.I. Nightingales: The Army Nurse Corps in World*

*War II*. Lexington, KY: The University Press of Kentucky, 1996.

Treadwell, Mattie E. *United States Army in World War II: The Women's Army Corps*. Washington, D.C.: Department of the Army, 1954.

Watkins, T.H. *The Great Depression: America in the 1930s*. Boston: Little, Brown and Company, 1993.

Williams, Denny. *To the Angels*. San Francisco: Denson Press, 1985.

Winter, J.M. *The Experience of World War I*. New York: Oxford University Press, 1989.

## Pamphlets

Anderson, Charles R. *Papua: 23 July 1942-23 January 1943*. Washington D.C.: U.S. Army Center of Military History, CMH Pub 72-7, n.d.,

Andrade, Dale. *Luzon: 15 December 1944-4 July 1945*. Washington, D.C.: U.S. Army Center of Military History, CMH Pub 72-28, n.d.

Bellafaire, Judith A. *The Army Nurse Corps*. Washington, D.C.: U.S. Army Center of Military History, CMH Pub 72-14, n.d.

Department of the Army. *Army Battle Casualties and Nonbattle Deaths in World War II*: Final Report: 7 December 1941 – 31 December 1946.

Drea, Edward J. *New Guinea: 24 January 1943-31 December 1944*. Washington, D.C.: U.S. Army Center of Military History, CMH Pub 72-9, n.d.

Feller, Lt. Col. Carolyn M., and Maj. Debora R. Cox, eds. *Highlights in the History of the Army Nurse Corps*. Washington, D.C.: U.S. Army Center of Military History, 2000.

Kirkpatrick, Charles E. *Defense of the Americas: The U.S. Army Campaigns of World War II*. Washington, D.C.: U.S. Army Center of Military History, n.d.

## Journals and Magazines

### SIGNED

Clarke, Alice R., R.N. "Thirty-seven Months as Prisoners of War." *The American Journal of Nursing*, 45 (1945), 342-345.

Davis, Dorothy. *"I Nursed at Santo Tomas, Manila." The American Journal of Nursing*, 44 (1944), 29-30.

Evans, Jessie Fant. "Release from Los Banos." *The American Journal of Nursing*. 45 (1945), 462-463.

Gimmestad, Ella. "Red Cross Nursing Service and the 'Gripsholm.'" *The American Journal of Nursing*, 44 (1944), 31-32.

Hohf, Josephine. "Somewhere in Australia." *The American Journal of Nursing*, 45 (1945), 42-43.

Hunt, Frazier. " 'Ma' Clement and Her Guinea Girls." *Cosmopolitan*, September 1944, pp. 54-5, 145-6.

McFadzean, Andrew. "Interviews with Robert Bowie: The Use of Oral Testimony in Writing the Biography of Professor Robert Richardson Bowie, Washington Policy Planner and Harvard University Professor." *The Oral History Review*, 26 (1999), 29-46.

Mecca, Jo-Anne. "'Neither Fish, Flesh, Nor Fowl': The World War I Army Nurse." *Minerva: Quarterly Report on Women and the Military*, XIII (Summer 1995), 1-19.

Nicol, Brian. "Schofield Barracks." *Honolulu*, November 1981, pp- 94-95.

Norman, Elizabeth M., and Sharon Eifried. "How Did They All Survive?An Analysis of American Nurses' Experiences in Japanese Prisoner-of-War Camps." *Nursing History Review* (1995), 105-127.

Sarnecky, Col. Mary T. "Julia Catherine Stimson: Nurse and Feminist." *IMAGE: Journal of Nursing Scholarship*, 25 (Summer 1993 ), 113-119.

Sutherland, Dorothy. "Army War Show." *R-N*, October 1942, 22ff.

Warren, Tom. "Hallowed Ground." *The Washingtonian*, June 1999, pp. 52-57.

## UNSIGNED

"Army Nurses at Leyte." *The American Journal of Nursing*, 45 (1945), 44.

"I'd Take Combat Duty Again." *The American Journal of Nursing*, 44 (1944), 676.

"Knollwood Celebrates 35 Years of Caring for the Military Community." *Bugle Call*, Winter 1997. The Army Distaff Foundation, Inc., Washington, D.C.

"News About Nursing: Soldiers' Medal." *The American Journal of Nursing*, 43 (1943), 774.

"Another Nurse Wins the Soldiers' Medal." *The American Journal of Nursing*, 43 (1943), 959.

# Newspapers

## SIGNED

Johnson, Dorothy. "Women in War Work." *Chicago Tribune*, July 1944.

Tousignant, Marylou. "VOICES: Nola Forrest: 'Oh, for a skirt again, just to flirt again — in a skirt again.'" *The Washington Post*, 26 July 1995.

White, Rex G. "The Army Pitches a Town With Speed and Precision." *Detroit Free Press*, n.d.

## UNSIGNED

"'Angels of Bataan' All Accounted for." *The New York Times*, 6 February 1945.

"Bataan Nurses Start for Home." *The New York Times*, 14 February 1945.

"Coast Guard Captain Braves Fire to Rescue Wreck Victims." *The Washington Post*, 25 September 1942,

"Heroic Nurses Get Thanks of Nation." *The New York Times*, 27 February 1945.

"Marry or Not, They'll Stay in the Army, Nurses Told." *The Washington Post*, 26 September 1942.

"Nola G. Forrest, Army Nurse Officer." *The Washington Post*, 5 August 1999.

"Rail Crash Death Toll Set at 14; Prosecutor Checks Train Speed." *The Washington Post*, 26 September 1942.

"Rescued Nurses All Kept Health; Back in U.S.; Eager to Visit Folks." *The New York Times*, 26 February 1945.

"Riders Calm, Say Wreck Witnesses." *The Washington Post*, 25 September 1942.

"68 Bataan Heroines Arrive on 4 Planes." *The New York Times*, 25 February 1945.

"Sturdy Nurses Prove Myth of Weaker Sex," *Slayton Herald*, July 1943.

"20 Die in Blazing Wreck of 3 B. & O. Trains in Pass." *The New York Times*, 25 September 1942.

"Weaker Sex Theory Disproved in Desert." *The New York Times*, 9 October 1943.

# Anthologies

Hoffman, Alice M., and Howard 5. Hoffman. "Reliability and Validity in Oral History: The Case for Memory." *In Memory and History: Essays on Recalling and Interpreting Experience* (see above).

Linton, Marigold. "Phoenix and Chimera: The Changing Faces of Memory." In *Memory and History* (see above).

Loftus, Elizabeth F. "Tricked by Memory." In *Memory and History* (see above).

Nevins, Allan. "How We Felt About the War." In *While You Were Gone: A Report on Wartime Life in the United States.* (see above).

Norman, Elizabeth M. "They Had No Choice But to Survive." In *Critical Issues in American Nursing in the Twentieth Century: Perspectives and Case Studies.* Eds. Darwin H. Stapleton, and Cathryne A. Welch. Guilderland, NY: Foundation for the New York State Nurses Assn., 1994.

Pavri, Julie M. "New York Nurses and the National Nursing Council for War Service." In *Critical Issues in American Nursing in the Twentieth Century* (see above).

# Encyclopedias

## SIGNED

Massenger, Charles. *The Chronological Atlas of World War Two*. New York: Macmillan Publishing Company, 1989.

Ward, Patricia Spain. "Stimson, Julia Catherine." *Dictionary of American Biography: Supplement Four, 1946-1950*.

Weatherford, Doris. "Blanchfield, Florence Aby." *Dictionary of American Biography: Supplement Nine, 1971-1975*.

## UNSIGNED

"Fort Snelling." *The New Columbia Encyclopedia*. 1975 ed.

"Liberty Ships." *World War II: America at War, 1941-1945*. New York: Random House, 1991.

"Manila." *The New Columbia Encyclopedia*. 1975 ed.

"Papua New Guinea." *The New Columbia Encyclopedia*. 1975 ed.

"Philippines, Republic of the." *The New Columbia Encyclopedia*. 1975 ed.

"Schofield Barracks." *Encyclopedia of Historic Forts*.

"Stimson, Henry Lewis. *The New Columbia Encyclopedia*. 1975 ed.

"Wallace, De Witt." *Who's Who in America, 1968-1969*. Vol. 35.

"Wood, Leonard." *The New Columbia Encyclopedia*. 1975 ed.

# Unpublished Dissertation

Gaskins, Susanne Teepe. "G.I. Nurses at War: Gender and Professionalism in the Army Nurse Corps during World War II." Diss. Univ. of California, Riverside, December 1994.

# ACKNOWLEDGMENTS

This book is built on the contributions of many people. The basic source was the spoken narrative of Nola Forrest saved on audio tape and interview notes, and her personal account was buttressed by information in books, articles, interviews, and official documents, including her papers. Yet only through the encouragement and special knowledge of a number of individuals could her story have been properly told.

First, I wish to thank two people whose enthusiasm from the beginning kept me energized. One was Maj. Constance Moore (now LTC), the Army Nurse Corps Historian in 1995 and 1996, who gave me the first sense of the way the role of Army nurses had been perceived and the way the perception had changed. She steered me to a number of essential documents, answered innumerable questions, and reviewed early versions of the text. The other was my first editor, Barbara Scheiber, whose tactful corrections and suggestions helped to shape my language over endless revisions of the manuscript. She believed the story held interest even when long stretches of the narrative had gone flat.

The process continued under the guidance of a number of endlessly helpful people in the Army Center of Military History. These included a series of Army Nurse Corps Historians who followed one another's 2-year tours of duty over a 10-year period. They combed the ANC files for bios, first-hand accounts, statistics, and pictures, often finding relevant material I could not have known existed. These were Lt. Col. Iris West, Lt. Col. Faye Hatter, Lt. Col. Debulon E. Bell, and Lt. Col. Cynthia F. Brown. They were followed by Maj. Debora R. Cox, Maj. Jennifer L. Petersen, and Lt. Col. Charlotte Scott relocated in the Office of the Surgeon General.

I am also indebted to Mary Ellen Condon-Rall, co-author of the official Army history, *Medical Service in the War Against Japan*. She explained the relationship between different levels of the SWPA medical command and steered me to Pauline Maxwell's redoubtable unpublished "History of the Army Nurse Corps, 1775-1948." She and the nurse history staff members provided information that was indispensable to the narrative, and I am grateful for their help.

At different stages I lent my manuscript for review to people with special knowledge. One was Brig. Gen. Connie L. Slewitzke (Ret.), chief of the Army Nurse Corps from 1983 to 1987, whose careful reading corrected several misconceptions and actual misstatements and emphasized the importance of source notes. Another was Dr. Linda Grant DePauw, founder of *Minerva*, the only journal on women and the military, and noted author on women and war. She helped to place the story in a firmer historical context. Other reviewers included Lt. Col. Patricia Jernigan (Ret.), who reminded me of the importance of citing, in order, the legislative actions that embodied the growing status of the Army Nurse Corps within the military and within women's history; also Dorothy Schneider, oral historian and co-author with her husband Carl of books on modern military women. I deeply appreciate the comments of all these reviewers who contributed so much to the reliability of my text.

Later on I was able to interview Brig. Gen. Anna Mae Hays, superintendent and subsequently chief of the Army Nurse Corps from 1967 to 1971. She knew Nola Forrest personally and could provide a sense of the relative informality of nursing administration in earlier days against the rules and regulations that prevail today. She also found me another former SWPA nurse to interview, and this enriched the story.

I wish to thank Robert Aarons, who made his mother's papers available and later donated them to the ANC archives. Erma Myers Aarons, wrote letters home from the Pacific and kept a diary that provided a lively contrast between the experiences of a bedside Army nurse and those on administrative levels.

I also wish to thank Maxine Russell for permission to quote from *Jungle Angel: Bataan Remembered*, her memoir of Lt. Col. Hortense McKay, who served in the Pacific and knew Colonel Forrest. Thanks are due to Kate Scott, oral historian of WIMSA (Women in Military Service for America), for offering a transcript of the memories of another Army nurse who served in the SWPA region.

Professional assistance was provided by several people who gave the book its final shape. One of these was Sue Shoenberg, my editor, who showed me how to bring my character to life and vary my language. Another was Chris Robinson, experienced map maker. Still another was Jay, computer coach, who patiently led me through the frustrations of Microsoft Word when my old word processor had become obsolete and I feared my project had ground to a halt. I want to thank the Still Pictures Branch of the National Archives for willing help on finding pictures. I am most grateful for the cooperative spirit of Adele Robey, book designer par excellence.

Last and not least I owe the origins of this undertaking to Dr. Robert B. Forrest, nephew of Nola Forrest, who provided me with copies of her papers, lent encouragement all along the line, and even wrote part of the final chapter detailing the travels of her great grandfather and his kin.

It takes a village to write a book.